Passport
To
Perfection

David Torkington

This book is dedicated to those first described by St Peter as 'The People of God', and to their spiritual growth and advancement

"There is only One way to perfection and that is to Pray. If anyone points in another Direction then they are deceiving you." St Teresa of Avila

Mercier Press, 82c Ballyhooly Road, St. Luke's, Cork, Ireland

Published by Mercier Press, 2025
Copyright © David Torkington, 2024

MERCIER PRESS

ISBN: 9781917453493

Cover design by Kelsey A. Moreau

David Torkington has sold over 450,000 books and been translated into 12 languages.

He is the author of:

- Inner Life – A Fellow Traveller's Guide to Prayer
- A New Beginning – A Sideways Look at the Spiritual Life
- Never too Late to Love – Our Lady's Sublime Teaching on Prayer
- Early Christian Spirituality
- How to Pray – A Practical Guide to the Spiritual life
- The Primacy of Loving – The Spirituality of the Heart
- Wisdom from The Western Isles – The Making of a Mystic
- Wisdom from Franciscan Italy – The Primacy of Love
- Wisdom from the Christian Mystics – How to Pray the Christian Way
- Dear Susanna - It's Time for a Christian Renaissance

These books have been listed in order of their readability, but they are all easily accessible to the general reader. The more you read them, the deeper you enter into the mystery of Christ, who is the Alpha and the Omega, the beginning and the end of the journey upon which the reader of this book has embarked. A *Passport to Perfection* is a practical companion to David's free course on Prayer at: https://www.essentialistpress.com.

David Torkington's website: https://www.davidtorkington.com

Biblical references are from The Jerusalem Bible 1966 edition

The Passport Monogram

> *"You must therefore be perfect, just as your*
> *heavenly Father is perfect."*   *(Matthew 5:48)*

Most passports carry some sort of insignia or sign, a crest or coat of arms on the cover, to show where the bearer comes from and who is guaranteed to support them on their journey. For this passport we have chosen an ancient Catholic monogram of the Holy Name of Jesus. It is He who makes this journey possible in the first place, and it is He who guarantees to support us on 'The Way' to perfection, to the perfect love that resides in God His Father. His Father sent Him to bring us to the place where His perfect Love will be our reward in the Kingdom without end, for which He created us. We have seen this monogram many times, and in different forms, but so few of us actually understand where it came from and how it came to be formed, even though we know to whom it refers. Let me explain.

When the ancient Jews gave a person a name, that name was meant to define their identity and their purpose, who they were, and what they did. That is why when God finally told His people His name, He told them that it is Love. When St John said that God is Love, he was only repeating what Jesus Himself told him and the other Apostles. That is, what He is in Himself as well as what He does. Notice that this name is not a noun but a verb - God is both love and loving at the same time. We do not have a tense in the English language to help us appreciate precisely what this means, but the 'present continuing tense' in the Irish language does. It means that God has loved us, is loving us, and will continue to love us forever.

In order to tell us this and explain what it means for us, God sent us His only son Jesus, who was, and still is the flesh and blood embodiment of His infinite loving. This means that all who were and all who still are open to receive His son's love, will receive the self-same life and Love that animates Him now. This love can save us all from enthralment with the selfishness and sinfulness that is the cancer of the soul and the greatest threat to the journey that we have undertaken. That is why God insisted that His son be called Jesus, which means 'The one who saves us, the deliverer, or the Saviour', because only His love can do what nothing else can do. That is why His holy name is the most powerful name on earth as St Paul tells us (Philippians 2:10-11). It should not be surprising then that it was made into and constantly used as a prayer in the early Church ultimately coming to be called the Jesus Prayer. Repeating this prayer in its shortest form, as taught by Abbot Macarius, came to be used as a special act of devotion and was particularly championed by St Bernard and eventually by the Dominican and Franciscan schools of spirituality.

However, it was with St Bernadine of Siena (1380-1444) and his fellow Franciscan reformers of the fifteenth century that this devotional practice took off in a major way. He told the hundreds of thousands of his followers to enshrine the word Jesus on their hearts and continually recite it with their tongues, but lest they forget to do this to do something else too. The abbreviation for the Greek word for Jesus, IHS (Ihsous), was used by ancient scribes. For St Bernadine it became a monogram or Christogram that he encouraged them to place in and outside of their churches, public buildings, and inside and outside their own homes, as tourists can still see all over Italy to this day. The genius of this short prayer is that it can be just as helpful to complete beginners on their spiritual journey as it can be to those advanced in the mystic way.

This short prayer is particularly helpful when the spiritual life deepens, and the journey upon which we have embarked encounters distractions, temptations, and dark nights that threaten to make us turn back, or even give up the journey completely. In times like this, the simpler the prayer the better. What better prayer to make than this; calling on His name for help, in good times and in hard times when all seems to be well or when everything seems to be falling apart. Then, when mystical purification is at its height and only a single word is as much as a person can muster, what more appropriate word can be used as a prayer for spiritual succour and support than the Holy Name of Jesus. Towards the end of her life, when my mother was lying in bed seriously ill with her rosary beads in her hand, she was almost in tears. She told me she could no longer say her favourite prayer. All she could say was the single word, the simplest and most powerful of all prayers, the Holy Name of Jesus. When, after her death I told my Father about her tears, he said they were not tears of pain but of joy. He said she was never more joyful at the end of her life than at any other time.

After the Renaissance and the decline of the Greek language in favour of Latin, the IHS came to be used as an acronym for the Latin,

'Jesus Hominum Salvator', meaning 'Jesus Saviour of Humankind'. The three nails used to fix Jesus to the Cross were then added to the monogram, and a small cross was mounted on the letter 'H'. There is no letter 'J' in the Greek alphabet and that is why the letter 'I' (iota) was used to write the first letter of the holy name, a practice that remained after the Latin came to be used in the new acronym.

However, lest we should forget, our redemption did not end with His death on the Cross, but with His glorification, so the monogram was set in a circle of fire. The circle of fire represents the Sun which from the earliest times was seen as a symbol of the Resurrection and glorification of Jesus. The flames that radiate from the perimeter are meant to be a continual reminder of the unquenchable fire of love that Jesus first released upon us all on the first Pentecost day and on every subsequent day for those who are open to receive it.

When you recite the word 'Jesus' as the prayer *par excellence*, you need say no more. The One who hears your prayer hears your deepest needs that Jesus came to satisfy, even though you may not realise what they are yourself, and so cannot find words to express them. When you are in trouble and the whole world seems to have conspired against you, do not think you have to explain your plight to the One who knows anyway; just say the 'Jesus Prayer'. When you are in the blackest moment of the 'Dark Night of the Soul' and the very gates of hell seem to be open to engulf you, just say the 'Jesus Prayer'. It is not a mantra, but the most powerful prayer of all and a prayer which will always be answered because as Jesus promised at the Last Supper, anything you ask of God in His name will be granted (John 16:23-24). When I asked a contemporary contemplative how he prayed, he said, "I use the Holy Name followed by the words of St Thomas, 'My Lord and My God' and then the prayer of St Francis, 'My God and My All', which is the motto of the Franciscan order. But the prayer I use most is the Holy Name, until Love's response is savoured in Silence".

If you persevere on your spiritual journey to Perfect Love, this prayer will gradually lead you into the prayer of experience, when what was asked for in darkness will be received in light. It is the light of the same love that raised Jesus from the dead that will raise us from the dead too, from the tomb that we have made for ourselves through sin and selfishness. This light will enable us to rise in, with, and through Jesus, drawing us up and into His all-engrossing and totally enthralling loving of God. It is here that we are filled with the fruits of contemplation where Jesus can continue to do again through us what He first did Himself whilst He was on earth and did again through the Apostles and those who followed Him after His Resurrection. What a perfect monogram for our passport to Perfect Love.

Foreword

In the life of grace, one seeks to remain open to the Presence of God gently knocking at the door of one's heart so as to respond with *fiat*. Is it by chance or by the goodness of the Lord that I happened to stumble across one of Mr Torkington's videos from Essentialist Press? The video captivated me. Ever desirous of developing a deeper level of prayer in my daily commitment as a priest, Mr Torkington's historical understanding of contemplative prayer in the Catholic Church, and his own practice of it as expressed in the entirety of his life, led me to pay attention and make a definitive decision to listen to what he had to say. His engaging appeal reminds me of St Francis Xavier writing about his desire to tour the great universities of Europe instilling in men a greater desire to charity and service to the missions. In this case, however, it is Mr Torkington crying out to Christians of this age, that we are missing a vital stepping stone that would bear greater fruit in our Christian lives and ultimately Holy Mother Church.

Having followed a number of videos, I began to express to my parishioners a desire to offer a series of lectures based on the reading of a book on prayer or perhaps the use of videos. In fact, on one morning, stopping after Friday morning Mass at our parish men's group, I mentioned to them that there is a man named Mr Torkington whose video series on contemplative prayer captivated me and I wanted to share such with our parish. Through a gift of Divine Providence, Mr Kevin Wells, who had written the foreword to Mr Torkington's latest book, *Family Spirituality* happened to be joining the men's group that particular morning. It was through him that I was able to come into contact with both Ryan Moreau and David Torkington, to welcome his teaching in a more profound way into my life and those of my beloved flock of parishioners.

With gratitude to the Lord and the message that Mr Torkington is sharing with so many people of good will desirous of a deep relationship with Our Lord, I wish to encourage Christians to delve into what he has to say about the intense prayer life of the first Christians and why it is not only accessible to us in this age, but necessary to recover in this moment in the life of our holy Church. *Passport to Perfection* offers the gift handed on by the Lord Jesus to the nascent Church - to be united to the One Sacrifice offered by Him on the cross and in His Resurrection, through our own daily sacrifices in the context of the celebration of the Holy Eucharist. A deeply reverent and prayerful celebration of the Holy Mass is prepared for by authentic prayer and union with Christ, that is, contemplation.

Mr Torkington has the wisdom of years of praying and uniting his own daily sacrifices to the Sacrifice of Christ in Holy Mass, to offer us not just encouragement, but an imperative that transcends the internal battles which plague our Church.

Fr Brian Welding

Contents

Part 1 Prayer

Part 2 Meditation

Part 3 Contemplation

Part 4 Sacrifice

Introduction

When I went to bed at night, the house was completely blacked out. When I woke in the middle of the night, it was to rush into the air raid shelter with the rest of the family. We never stopped saying the rosary until the siren sounded the 'all clear'. I was often cold and hungry for fuel, and food was short. I was used to wearing hand-down clothing because you needed precious coupons to buy new. There was no sport to divert us at weekends, for all the players had been called up to fight for King and country. Where we went, who we spoke to and what we did was all restricted. It was a strange world, but it was not strange to me. I was born shortly before the second world war started, and what was new and all but unbearable to everyone else in the family was simply normal to me. I took this strange new world for granted for I knew no other, much like Catholics today. They have grown up in a strange religious world, yet they have known no other, and think it is normal, just as I thought the war years were normal. Yet, it is aeons away from the first Catholic world and the faith that was first introduced by Jesus Christ Our Lord.

The first lines of L.P Hartley's book *The Go-Between*, are, "The past is a foreign Country - They do things differently there". They did things differently at the dawn of our faith that we have all but forgotten. It was a world dominated by the Resurrection of Jesus Christ Our Lord, the sending of His Holy Spirit and the first flowering of the faith under His ongoing spiritual providence. That is why we must return to that time, at least in spirit, to recover what we have lost and readapt it to a world that has long since been spiritually bankrupt, and our lives with it.

Immediately after the Ascension, Our Lady, the Apostles, and the first disciples would have been all but totally bereft if Jesus had not promised to send His Holy Spirit in the near future, to remain with them, this time from the inside through Love. When He finally came on the first Pentecost day, Our Lady and the Apostles and the first converts were immediately transformed, but some were more transformed than others. Because there was no sin in her, Our Lady was instantly taken up into her beloved son. Before the first Christmas Day, her son was in her womb, but now on the first Pentecost Day she was in Him, in His new mystical Body. She had attained what later mystical writers in the West came to call the Mystical Marriage or the Spiritual Marriage, or what was called in the Eastern Church, *Theosis*. They called it *Theosis*, because in, with, and through her beloved son, she was now open to contemplate God in Himself, embodied in the Three in One. There, she received in return for her lifelong loving what the Fathers of the Church called the *Pleroma*, the cornucopia of the Father's love. In this Love she received what her beloved son received throughout His life on earth. That is, what

St Thomas Aquinas would call Contemplation and the fruits of Contemplation.

By the fruits of contemplation, he meant, all the infused Theological, Cardinal, and Moral virtues together with the gifts and fruits of the Holy Spirit. Just as a shaft of colourless light carries within it all the colours of the spectrum, so God's Love carries within it all the infused virtues, all the gifts, and all the fruits of His Love. Then, just as they all become visible for all to see when they strike a prism, so God's supernatural gifts can be seen when they strike a loving human heart, to be reflected and refracted in all they say and do. When this love struck the loving heart of Mary it enabled her to become the Mother He asked her to become, shortly before He died on the cross. She became a mother, not just to St John, but to the infant Church until the first Apostles and disciples too, had sufficiently received the fruits of Contemplation for themselves, to bring God's Kingdom of Love to the Pagan Roman world that Love would conquer.

That the Apostles were still sinners is obvious to anyone who has read the Gospels. Yes, they too had received the Holy Spirit on that first Pentecost Day; however, it would take years in retreat at Jerusalem before they could receive the fruits of the Contemplation that they now had to prepare to receive in darkness and in light until they were ready and prepared for their apostolic mission to the world. There were a myriad of others who received the Holy Spirit on that day, but they were total beginners and in receiving the Holy Spirit they were touched only superficially at first. Their emotions and their feelings were overwhelmed by receiving the Holy Spirit so suddenly. Inevitably and understandably, they began to express their feelings. When such feelings are experienced in a group, then they begin to manifest striking psychosomatic phenomena similar to group experiences in subsequent centuries as described in Monsignor Ronald Knox's book, *Enthusiasm*.

That is why modern members of the Charismatic Renewal are correct when they point to the first Christians as their legitimate antecedents. However, there was an important difference, which they would be advised to note if they would grow as the first Charismatic Christians grew, from spiritual adolescence to spiritual maturity as full blown saints and martyrs. As they were predominantly Jews, they already practised a daily routine of prayer that began first thing in the morning and ended last thing at night. Then they prayed further, and in public, three times a day in the synagogue, or in the temple, at least as long as it stood. Even when the Jewish authorities decided to 'excommunicate' them, they continued to pray in private, as their mothers had taught them, and 'in public' in one anothers' homes. From the start they were taught another form of prayer called Meditation, that I will deal with more fully later. As so many of them had only heard about, but never seen their Messiah, those who had would tell them about Him in detail around the fire side and at their weekly Mass. Often, two or three speakers who had known Christ would enthrall their congregations with stories about the most lovable man who had ever lived. Then they were taught to go away and meditate on all they had learned so that they would be led on from meditating on Christ, as he had once been on earth, to contemplating Him, as He is now in heaven. If the leadership of modern Charismatics had done likewise, then six or more decades that have been wasted could have been deeply fruitful, and we could now be led by worthy successors of the Apostles. However, Charismatics are still with us and in large numbers. If only their leaders would do for them what Our Lady and the first Apostles did for their antecedents, then the Church would be more than strong enough to be a match to the satanic secularism that is threatening to destroy us. However, it is not too late. The raw materials for contemplative apostles are still with us now, and it is the time to prepare them to become the saints that we need to lead us.

All too often in the past, pseudo-spiritual writers who have designed their own weird and wonderful spiritualities or gimmicky ways to instant sanctity, have projected them into the past to give them legitimacy. They have done this in such a way that their own creations seem to be canonised by our illustrious and saintly forebears. Or they cherry pick from quotations taken out of context to prove their heresies. For over five decades now, good Catholics who are serious searchers have been bamboozled by modern pseudo-mystics who offer instant contemplation, not as taught by Authentic Catholic mystics from the beginning, but by Eastern Gurus belonging to a tradition at serious odds with that which has come down to us from Jesus Christ. He did not teach mantras as the way to perfection, but rather the Cross, carried daily in imitation of Him. It is here where true self-sacrifice is learnt that leads to the practice of divine love that alone leads to union with God and the contemplation through which He gives all the infused virtues and gifts of the Holy Spirit. The way they ensnare good people into seeking instant mysticism by the recitation of mantras is positively evil. Practitioners may find a certain instant psychological satisfaction as they learn to sedate their minds for a time with what amounts to be mental forms of yoga, often used as an aid for patients suffering from mental stress, but they are millions of miles away from authentic Catholic contemplative prayer. Those who have been promoting this nonsense have proclaimed their own spiritual emptiness and betrayed the tradition to which they belong. That many of these have been monks on both sides of the Atlantic, is yet one more example of why we are all in such a state of spiritual bankruptcy. I have been scrupulous in what follows, to detail only what is the God-given Spirituality that Jesus Christ Our Lord first lived Himself before introducing it to the early Church. I have been as honest and as accurate as possible, to show how this spirituality can be legitimately adapted to the modern world, to do again what the first Christians did for the ancient pagan world.

When, as a boy, I decided to study and practise Judo, I bought a book detailing how to master the sport. Although I read it at a sitting in one evening, it took me three years of daily hard work before I could attain a black belt. You can read this little book at a sitting but believe me it will take more than three years before you can come anywhere near to putting it into practice as the early Christians did. I bought a similar sort of book when I decided to study Chess to become a grandmaster. I learnt several wonderful ideal openings that would give me a head start on everyone else. However, I never managed to complete any of them, because there was always an opposition that had other ideas. I have tried to detail the spiritual ideals in this book, but sadly, and as you know, there is an opposition who is at work trying to destroy any ideals that you try to put into practice, so, be on your guard, and never be discouraged when you falter, fail, or fall. The secret of the spiritual life is that it is all in the getting up when you have failed or fallen. It is not so much the pride that comes before the fall that is our enemy, but the pride after the fall that prevents us from getting up time and time again. The difference between us and the saints is not that they did not fall and we do, but rather the speed with which they have the humility to keep getting up, time and time again.

The Jewish Philosopher Simone Weil said that, "We are no more than the quality of our endeavour". That we will fall is certain, but what matters to God is how best we try, and how best we keep trying, no matter how many times we fall. That is how God will ultimately judge us, by how best we have tried, in the context of the cards that we have been dealt at the beginning of our journey. There is an old Spanish proverb that says, "You see what I drink but you do not see my thirst". God does. Thank God for God!

David Torkington

Part 1 Prayer

Chapter 1

The Journey Ahead

Before I begin to speak about prayer, let me make a few observations about the journey ahead. The journey upon which the traveller is about to depart is not a day trip, nor is it a brief excursion, or even a long sabbatical. It is a journey that begins here and now, from here to eternity. Our Guide has said that those who seriously set out, but turn back, are not fit for His Kingdom of Love, because they stop looking where they are going and begin looking where they came from, to the world of self-indulgence where they started. Someone once said that happiness is a journey from selfishness to selflessness. How true, as the traveller who perseveres on this journey will soon find out. One of the best psychological antidotes to depression that so many of us suffer today as we view the contemporary world is called 'cognitive therapy', in which we continually try to replace depressive and spiritually debilitating thoughts with good or pleasant ones. What better thought to begin with than that the One who created the world did so with no other objective than for us to share in His own infinite bliss and eternal happiness for all eternity. He is 'The Way', and that is why the expression 'The Way' was used to describe the first Christian travellers. The journey back home began at the first Pentecost when He sent His love, the Holy Spirit, to draw all who wished to be taken up within Him. That journey begins in earnest for us anew when we take up this passport and use it to help us travel from here to Eternity.

However, it is important to make it clear that the journey which begins in the person of Jesus Christ, leads us in, with, and through Him, to first contemplate the Glory of the God who created us, and then to travel onwards into the Glory of God, who is the perfection of endless loving for which we yearn.

We are called to do our best to love God as Jesus did. But how do we begin? We begin by realising that God is only to be found in Jesus Christ, and it is in trying to love Him that we come to know and love God. Remember Christ's words to St Philip at the Last Supper: "Do you not believe that I am in the Father and the Father is in Me?" Our journey then is not so much into outer space, but into inner space, where God is to be found by coming to know and love Christ.

A famous Benedictine Abbot, William of Saint-Thierry, who was a close personal friend of St Bernard of Clairvaux said, "You cannot love someone unless you know them, but you will never really come to know them unless you love them." He then applied this principle to coming to know and love God in Jesus Christ. We have been sadly living for all too long in a world where there is no lack of knowledge about God. Tens of thousands of people have studied theology, but so very few have come to love God as the first Christians did in the early Church, or as our forefathers did three or four hundred years ago. There are two main types of Theology: Systematic and Mystical Theology. Systematic Theology primarily exercises the mind, and Mystical Theology primarily exercises the heart.

Ninety-nine percent of readers are unaware that Mystical Theology, that was specifically the making of the saints, was outlawed after almost sixteen hundred years. This occurred when a heinous heresy - one that perverted true Catholic Mystical Theology and condoned serious sexual sins - was condemned with its founder, a Spanish Secular Priest called Molinos, operating out of Rome in 1687. Since then, Contemplation, the prayer that Christ Himself practised every day of His life, and taught to others has virtually been forgotten. It must return, and return without delay, for as St Thomas Aquinas said, "With contemplation all things become possible, and without it nothing becomes possible". All the Theological Virtues, the Cardinal Virtues, and the Moral virtues, not to mention the gifts and fruits of the Holy Spirit that we see redolent in the life of Christ and the great saints, are denied to us without the gift of contemplation. In the aftermath of the heresy of Quietism, contemplation was taken away. Any form of prayer that could lead to contemplation, such as meditation, was either outlawed or discouraged. If nonetheless individuals persevered, there was no one to guide them into and through the contemplation that was commonplace in the early Church. That is why, without the supernatural life and love given in contemplation, the Church that we know and love has been scandalising the world as it descends into ever greater degeneracy. Most people know about the terrible heresy of Arianism in the early Church, but the aftermath of Quietism has been, and still is much worse, and perhaps worst of all for hardly anyone has even noticed it.

We must now follow the lead of St John Henry Newman and go back to study and practise the simple theology of the early Church, where theology and mystical theology were hardly distinguishable.

For the first Christians, to know someone meant to love them, and it was the love that they received from God in return for loving and contemplating Him that was decisive. It made the first Christians redolent, resplendent, and radio-active with the love of God. It was the fruits of Contemplation that enabled them to transform a pagan Roman Empire into a Christian Empire in such a short time. Almost every early Catholic committed to his or her faith was in fact a theologian and a mystical theologian at one and the same time. A famous and learned monk called Evagrius Ponticus who synthesised the spiritual teaching of the early monks said, "A theologian is a person of prayer, and a person of prayer is a theologian". When that can be said once more, then the New Spring that St John Henry Newman promised will be well underway. This *Passport to Perfection* and the prayer life that will gradually unfold within it, has been taken from the profound and sublime spiritual teaching taught by the Holy Spirit to our first Catholic forebears. It is this teaching that I have been at pains to lay before you, that can help us begin again today to do in our day what the Holy Spirit did through them in their day.

Chapter 2

Context and Our Destination

In the Lord's Prayer, Christ gave us the pattern of all prayer. The first two words, 'Our Father', sum up the rest of the prayer and are the key to understanding the basic context and direction of all Christian prayer. Our trouble is that familiarity has anaesthetised our minds, dulling our intellects so that the depth of meaning with which these words are charged simply passes us by.

Take the word OUR. This one word sums up the whole context of all prayer. Prayer lifts us up out of ourselves and gradually takes us more deeply into Christ into whom we were drawn up at Baptism. In Him we are drawn into the total community of all those who are alive and loving Him here and now.

The Gospel is the story of what happens to those who open themselves totally to the power of uncreated love which leads them to perfection in Christ, when our weak human love finally becomes filled with the infinite power of God's Love. The Resurrection shows the inevitable consequences of this process in the life of Christ. It also makes it quite clear that what happened to Him will happen to all who are prepared to follow Him, to do what He did. His Resurrection means that those who continually open themselves to love, come what may, will in the end be possessed by it. As this process reaches its climax, we will be lifted out of ourselves into a new mode of being altogether. We can see this happening to Christ at the end of the Gospel story. The Resurrection pinpoints the moment in time when Christ is so possessed by love that He is raised up outside of time into a new form of existence, beyond all the laws and limitations of the space-and-time world to which we belong and into which He was born.

Before the Resurrection, Jesus was subject to all the restrictions that bind the rest of us. He too could only be in one place at any given moment. Contact with Him therefore was necessarily limited to where He happened to be, how long He was going to stay there and how many other people wanted to see Him. Once love had lifted Him out of the world of space and time, however, He was freed from all those limiting laws and restrictions. In the eternal dimension, He could be present to countless numbers of people at any given moment because He could be present to them, not from the outside, but from the inside, through love. Now, He was not just the 'Man for all Seasons', but the man for all times, for all ages, for all generations simultaneously. This is why He is sometimes called the Eternal Contemporary. And since Christ can come into contact with everyone through love, then everyone can contact each other in Him. Just as the spokes of a wheel automatically come closer to one another as they draw nearer to the centre, so everyone automatically comes closer to one another as they draw nearer to Christ. The Kingdom of Love is the only place where genuine community really exists. It is here, in, with, and through Him that we begin our journey to perfect love. As the journey unfolds and we pray in, with, and through Him, then we draw closer and closer to Him so that in, with, and through Him, we can become more and more open to the Father whose infinite loving will finally totally possess us and make us perfect in Him. Here, all our deepest hopes and desires will find their fulfilment and completion.

However, always remember that when we say, 'Our Father', we do not just mean that we pray with Christ and in Him, but also that we pray together with all our brothers and sisters who are alive in Him, with the whole Christian community living or dead, because in Him there is no death. We pray with Mary too, with Peter and Paul, with Francis and Dominic, and all the saints. We pray with loved ones now dead, who have been reborn in Christ. When we pray with them, their prayer helps keep our supreme prayer united with God and His perfect love on track, despite the many distractions and temptations that try to turn our hearts and minds elsewhere.

This is why the first word of the Lord's Prayer is OUR. There is no place for the self-conscious 'I'. It is OUR Father, who art in heaven, hallowed be Thy Name, Thy kingdom come, Thy will be done, on earth as it is in heaven. Give US this day, OUR daily bread, and forgive US OUR trespasses, as WE forgive those who trespass against US, and lead US not into temptation, but deliver US from evil.

The whole Christian prayer tradition follows this pattern of prayer and is exemplified perfectly in the liturgy of the Church. There is no such thing as private prayer for Christians, although they may be praying in solitary confinement. The context of prayer is so important, both theologically and psychologically, that we ought to begin prayer by mentally reminding ourselves of the all-embracing world into which we enter, of the vast community of believers with whom we are identifying ourselves, in Christ in His mystical body. The whole point of prayer is that it takes believers out of themselves into another world where they no longer live for themselves but for others, in a community that supersedes the barriers of space and time.

While the first word of the Our Father, OUR, puts us in the right context, the second word, FATHER points us in the right direction. The Gospels show how it is the Holy Spirit who progressively invades and fires the human personality of Jesus, until he is eventually set ablaze with the love that raises Him irrevocably into the Father to Eternity. It is the flame of the same Spirit which radiates between the Father and the Son, that can reach out to us also, to fire us with the identical love that will enable all to be drawn into the community of their life.

Christ teaches us to call God 'Father' when we pray, because this is precisely what He is to us now. The actual word Jesus uses is even more telling than the translation to which we have become accustomed. He did not in fact use the word that is the equivalent to our word 'Father'. Instead, he chose the word *Abba.* This Aramaic word actually means 'Daddy', or at least the word 'Daddy' is the closest we can get to the original meaning. Christ's use of this familiar and homely pet name would have not only been new to his fellow Jews, but also shocking. I do not mean that God was never referred to as Father prior to this time. God had been called Father in the Old Testament on thirteen occasions. However, each time the word was employed, it was used as another word for creator. In other words, God was a Father in so far as he was responsible for His own handicraft, in the sense that we would say Michaelangelo was the Father of his statue Moses because He carved it, or that Hippocrates was the Father of medicine, or that Herodotus was the Father of all History because he created the literary genre.

The traditional word for Father, then, was already loaded with a meaning that Christ wished to supersede. The word *Abba* or 'Daddy', or its equivalent in any language, can only mean one thing. What is a daddy? Who is a daddy but one who communicates life to his children. There can be no misunderstanding as to what is meant by this word. The nuance is crucial for the new understanding that Christ wished to convey about God. God is now no longer to be understood merely as our Father, the One who created us, but the One who chooses to share His own life with us. This one word sums up the fullness of the Gospel message. That, if we only allow the same Spirit of love that entered into the life of Jesus to enter into our lives too, then we will be able to share not only in His life, but also in His action, in His love of the Father and in the Father's love of Him.

By faith we know that God is Our Father, but it is only when that faith grows and ripens in prayer that we actually start to experience God's love progressively entering into us as we pray to Him, in, through, and with Christ. It is not enough just to accept the bald and undeniable fact that God is a Father. If this truth is to change our lives, which it can, then it must be translated into an experience. This can only happen if we put aside the time daily to create the space in which to allow God to become a loving Father to us. We can prevent this happening, and the truth of the matter is, we do, repeatedly. We never seem to have the time. There is always something else that is more important, something that simply has to be done. Until we come to realise that there is nothing more important than allowing God to be a Father, and let Him enter our lives through prayer, then we can never be changed deeply and will never be able to change others either. Unless we allow God to touch us with His fatherly love, we may just as well call Him Ra, Jupiter, or Zeus, for all the practical difference He will make to our lives. This is why Jesus made it clear that the one condition necessary to enter into the Kingdom of God's love, is to become like a little child, so that He can become a Father to us.

We can all be sentimental about children and romanticise their innocent and simple goodness, but in reality they can be self-centred, greedy little mites. Jesus was not a romantic sentimentalist when it came to children. He was aware of their shortcomings and makes this quite clear when He castigates the Pharisees for acting like children, squabbling with each other on the street corners. But whatever the faults of little children, they have one redeeming feature that we cannot resist. They are irresistibly helpless and unable to manage for themselves. They have no illusions about their own strength; they are weak and incompetent, and they make no bones about it. If there is anything that becomes too much for them, be it an untieable shoelace or a dribbling nose, they run to Mummy or Daddy. They are utterly and completely dependent on their parents, and they do not care who knows it. This is the characteristic that Jesus is pointing to, when He says we must become as little children if we want to enter the Kingdom of Heaven.

Who is going to belittle themselves by getting down on their knees to pray unless they are first aware that they are in need of help? Without the basic humility of a little child, we cannot even begin. This is why Jesus says it is as difficult for a rich man to enter into the Kingdom of God as it is for a camel to pass through the eye of a needle. Jesus is not just referring to the person with a fat wallet or a big bank balance; He means people who are rich in natural gifts and abilities too, like the person with brains or flair, with administrative skills or business insight, with charm or artistic brilliance. None of these riches are evil in themselves, but they all have the same danger. They can so easily give a person a false impression of their own strength, their own importance and personal competence. Who needs God when money will get me all I want? Who needs God's help when I can do it myself? Riches of any sort obscure this fundamental vision that all of us need to have quite clearly in mind; namely, that we are basically weak and incapable of achieving anything lasting or worthwhile without God. We are totally dependent on Him for everything. If we do not see this we are blind, and we will stumble around for a lifetime and never find the right road, never mind enter the Kingdom.

All that I am trying to say revolves around a few simple truths that can alone lead us onwards to the perfect loving union with God, a union which we desire more than anything else. Namely, that the only power capable of changing us is love, and it is the experience of the Fatherly love of God which alone will radically change us deeply and permanently for the better. Next, our recognition of our own weakness is the only way we will come to feel our utter need of God's help. Third, building a life of prayer is the only logical step if we genuinely believe that we are completely dependent upon God. This means turning our lifestyle upside down, if need be, to find the necessary daily time for prayer, otherwise, we are just fooling ourselves and will go nowhere. Prayer is not just a luxury for priests or religious, or people who happen to have spare time on their hands. It is an absolute necessity for everyone who wants to plunge themselves effectively into the mystery of Christ's life and love, to see, and experience, in, with, and through Him, something of the Love of God. In this profound mystical contemplation is the prelude to the ecstatic and never-ending bliss that we experience as we are drawn ever more deeply into the infinite loving of God. St Paul tells us that this destiny for which God created us from the beginning is called the *Mysterion* from the Greek word meaning hidden, secret, or invisible. That is why those who chose to commit themselves to this journey gradually came to be called mystics, because their inner spiritual journey could not be seen by onlookers. It was hidden in Christ who was leading them to their ultimate destiny where their love would be brought to perfection in union with the Perfect love of Our Infinite God.

Now perhaps you can see what I mean by saying that the two words Our Father not only sum up the whole of the Lord's Prayer, but actually embody the basic context and direction of all authentic Christian prayer. The word OUR immediately sites our prayer in the centre of the Christian Community, which tradition calls the Community of Saints. In this community we are all bound to each other in Christ, inextricably set in a single direction, God-wards. We are inevitably drawn into the endless ecstasy of life and love that unceasingly surges out of the Son towards the Father, and we are filled to the measure of our weakness by the Father's richness. The more we are filled with His fullness, we are lifted up out of ourselves in a self-forgetfulness that enables us to pray properly for the first time. The more we are tangibly immersed in the mystery of God's love, the more we begin to see that all prayer leads to praise, to give glory to Him, and to lose ourselves in His inexhaustible goodness. The only petition that now seems to make sense is Hallowed be Thy Name, Thy Kingdom come, Thy will be done on earth as it is in heaven. From now on we begin to live for God alone. Suddenly everything else seems unimportant and trivial compared to living for Him.

Once we are plunged into the environment of God's love, our deepest yearnings reach out towards their fulfilment, and we know that nothing less than total immersion will satisfy us completely. Once we sense and experience, in some measure, the home for which we are destined, everything else pales into insignificance. The paltry pleasures that the world calls joy appear as dross to pure gold.

Chapter 3

Prayer and the Spiritual Life

Before giving you the practical details that will immediately enable you to start your journey to try and follow the way Christ prayed when He was on earth, let me remind you of one of the simplest and most accurate definitions of prayer which many will remember from their childhood. It is simply that, 'Prayer is the raising of our minds and hearts to God'. This means that whatever methods of prayer we may find helpful, they will get us nowhere if there is something fundamentally wrong with our attitude. Let me explain what I mean.

Two main attitudes have dominated the approach to God in prayer throughout the history of Christian spirituality. Before the Renaissance, the older religious orders emphasised the action of God, while the newer orders, founded after the rise of humanism, tended to emphasise the action of man. Both are orthodox, but both have inbuilt dangers that have often led people into a spiritual cul-de-sac.

Those who put all the emphasis on what God does can easily forget what they should be doing to cooperate with Him, thus falling into

Quietism. This leads to a sort of presumption as they present themselves to God in prayer like suet puddings waiting to be soaked in syrup! On the other hand, those who stress the importance of what we can do can forget what God does and can easily fall into what used to be called Pelagianism. They act as if everything depended on themselves. This can lead to a sort of spiritual pride, to an arrogance of heart and mind that destroys the prayer that they seem to believe depends more on their endeavour than on God's.

In order to avoid the danger of presumption, I would like to introduce the word "trying" into the traditional definition of prayer. Then, in order to avoid the danger of falling into pride, I would like to introduce the word "gently" to stress that our endeavour will lead us nowhere without God's help. If we get angry or upset at our failure, it is not because we have failed God, but because we have failed ourselves and the goal we thought we could attain by our own endeavour.

Prayer then is *gently trying* to raise the heart and mind to God. Despite having a perfect definition of prayer, most of us will spend much of our lives trying to walk the spiritual tightrope between pride and presumption, continually falling off, once this side then the other. Then in God's time, not ours, the Holy Spirit will eventually reward those of good will who have persevered despite human failures. They will finally receive the perfect balance that enables them to keep their hearts and minds open to God, free of the pride or presumption that can prevent them from receiving the love they long for more than anything else.

Despite what I have said, the spiritual life seems to have become so complicated over the years that you almost feel you need a couple of degrees in theology just to understand it before you can even attempt to live it. Yet it is essentially simple, so simple that you need the simplicity of a little child to see it. You see, there is only one thing that is necessary, and that is love. Not our love of God, but His love of us. In other words, Christianity is firstly a Mystical Theology, not a Moral Theology. It is not primarily concerned with detailing the perfect moral behaviour that we see embodied in Christ's life and then trying to copy it virtue by virtue. That is stoicism, not Christianity, and it is doomed to failure.

Christianity is primarily concerned with teaching us how to turn and open ourselves to receive the same Holy Spirit who filled Jesus Christ. The more we are filled with His love, the easier it is to return it in kind, as the divine suffuses and then surcharges human love so that it can reach up to God and out to others. Only then are we able to "love God with our whole hearts and minds and with our whole being and to love our neighbour as Christ loves us."(John 13:34).

The trouble is, we make the same mistake with Christ as we do with the saints. We read their lives backwards. We read about their rigorous lives, their superhuman sacrifices, and their heroic virtue, and we believe that the only way we can be like them is to do likewise. If we would only read their lives forward instead of backwards, then we would see that they were only capable of doing the seemingly impossible because they first received the power to do it from the Holy Spirit in prayer.

If we try to be and do what they did without first receiving what they received, then our brave attempts will inevitably end in disaster. True imitation of Christ or any of His saints means first copying the way they did all in their power to receive the Holy Spirit who inspired them. That is essentially all we have to do. That is why the spiritual life is so simple, if only we have the simplicity of a little child to see it. True imitation of Christ then means, not trying to replicate in our lives His exemplary dealings with others, not trying to love them as He did, not trying to acquire for ourselves all the Theological Virtues, the Cardinal Virtues, the Moral Virtues that we see Him exercising to perfection, but trying something that will give us the power to do all these things. Quite simply, this means to pray as He did, so that we can receive the Life and Love of the Holy Spirit who can make all things possible that are quite impossible without Him.

We know from the early Christian writings that Mary His mother taught Jesus to say His morning prayer each day. The prayer was called the *Shema*, and it was such an important prayer that it was said many times over each day when every good Jew would go to the Synagogue at nine o'clock, twelve o'clock, and three o'clock. This prayer embodies within it the first and greatest of the Commandments, which is to love God with your whole heart and mind, with your whole body and soul, and with your whole strength. As they practised this prayer, they would receive the help and strength of God to put into practice the second great Commandment which was to love others 'as you love yourself'. However lest I forget, remember that this second commandment was changed by Christ at the Last Supper to: "You must love others, not just as you love yourself, but as I have loved you" (John 13:34). So, by saying his *Shema* daily, Jesus offered up and consecrated the whole of the forthcoming day to God by promising to put into practice the most important two Commandments.

It was in putting this prayer into practice that Jesus was also putting into practice the new form of Worship that he promised to the Samaritan woman. As the days of the Old Temple were now finished, there would be a new way of offering Sacrifice to God; that is to offer oneself and all that we do each day. It would become a powerful new form of sacrifice because it would be offered up in the New Temple which was nothing other than His own mystical body.

In the next stage, I want to show how we can truly imitate Christ by following the example of how He prayed every day of His life. By praying as He prayed, because we pray in, with, and through Him, we can receive the same love of God that He received. In order to do this, I will transpose the *Shema* used by both Our Lord and Our Lady and all the apostles and disciples into what gradually came to be called the Morning Offering. By saying this and by trying to put both the first and the second Commandments into practice as Jesus did, we will receive as He did the fullness of the Holy Spirit who will enable us to do what Jesus Himself did, as He promised at the Last Supper.

Chapter 4

A Blueprint for Morning Prayer

The blueprint for daily prayer that follows is a modern Catholic reconstruction of the prayer that Our Lady herself was taught by her parents and which she taught her son, Jesus. After the sending of the Holy Spirit, she together with all the Apostles and new disciples, realised that henceforth they would always 'live and move and have their very being' in their Risen Lord, in his new and glorified mystical body, the New Temple. Here they would pray at all times, with and through Him. As he taught them, their new and ever-loving Divine Dad would be the object of their prayer and that is why the very prayer that He gave them, the 'Our Father', was the most commonly used communal and personal prayer.

Therefore, in order to introduce you to the new daily prayer life that Our Lady would have used together with His other disciples, I am going to use each letter of the Our Father for a blueprint to help you learn how to pray each day, as she did in her day, albeit with several accommodations using contemporary examples and the inspirations of the saints who have followed in her footsteps over the centuries.

The first three letters of the Our Father, O-U-R in the blueprint, will be a reminder of the three essential features of morning prayer. The letter -O- will be a reminder to say the morning offering in one form or another. The letter -U- will be a reminder that as we make this prayer, like Mary herself we are uniting ourselves with Christ her son and with all who are in Him. The letter -R- will be a reminder to review the coming day, resolving to do all and everything for the honour and glory of God. Then, every letter of the word Father could be used too, as a reminder of how to pray during the day at a time set aside for that purpose, or as night prayer.

The letter -F- will be a reminder to make an act of faith, enabling us to express our belief as simply as possible and in our own words, in the God who is an ever-loving Father, in Jesus his ever-loved and ever-loving Son, and in the Holy Spirit who draws us all back through Jesus into God's kingdom of endless loving. Once we have briefly meditated on what God has done for us and is continuing to do for us, it is time to make our response. To do this, the remaining letters of the word 'Father' can be used accordingly. The letter -A- stands for the word abandonment, -T- for thanksgiving, -H- for Holy Communion, -E- for examination of conscience, and finally -R- for repentance. To help beginners, I have included nine prayers that we can transpose into our own words to make more personal. These can be found in the addendum at the end of this book.

1. The Morning Offering

The letter 'O' can remind us to make our Morning Offering. For

Our Lady this morning offering was the *Shema* in which she offered the whole of the forthcoming day to God and promised to commit herself to loving God with her whole mind and heart, with her whole body and soul, and with her whole strength. We can do the same in our own way and in our own words, as Mary did the moment she woke in the morning. It was my mother who taught me to make my morning offering to dedicate the whole of the forthcoming day to God, to show that I loved Him with my whole being as Mary did, and to promise to try and show my love for Him throughout the day. My mother told me that by offering all I said and did to God in the day ahead of me, I could become, as she put it, a little priest turning ordinary commonplace things into something precious, as Rumpelstiltskin turned straw into gold. "You are a chosen race, a royal priesthood, a consecrated nation, a people set apart" (1 Peter 2:9).

When our family went to Mass each Sunday, we saw our mother totally absorbed in what we took all too easily for granted. Our selfishness meant we had too little to offer, while she was offering a thousand and one acts of self-sacrifice made for us during the previous week. Each day she reminded herself of this, her sacred calling, by making her Morning Offering as her recusant ancestors did for hundreds of years before her.

When Pope Benedict XVI was approached by a young couple who had five children and an extremely busy schedule feeding, clothing, and educating them each day, they asked him a question. It was a question they had been asking themselves, but to which they could find no answer. "How can we possibly find time for prayer?" they asked. "Our days are so full." They never forgot the Holy Father's answer. "By beginning each day with the Morning Offering, so that your whole life can become a prayer, just as the whole life of Jesus was a prayer, because He offered up everything He said and did to

His Father in heaven". If ever I forgot to say mine, my mother used to remind me that St Jean-Baptiste Vianney, the Curé d'Ars, would say, "All that we do without offering it to God, is wasted," and he was right. Let me give you a morning offering that I have used, although ideally you should use your own.

"God, our Father, I wish to consecrate all that I say and all that I do to you in this forthcoming day, just as Jesus did every day of His life on earth. Please accept what I do so imperfectly and unite it with the perfect offering that Jesus continues to make to you in heaven and in every Mass that is celebrated on earth. I offer to you my joys and my sorrows, my successes as well as my failures, because these especially show how much I have need of you. I make my prayer in, with, and through Jesus in whom we all live and move and have our being. Amen".

2. Union with Christ

Now for the letter -U-. It was my mother who first taught me something that Our Lady herself came to realise after her son's glorification. She said that even though I may make my morning offering alone by the side of my bed, I am not alone. My prayer is always made in, with, and through Jesus, and so with all other Christians, wherever they are. The great Jesuit liturgist Father Joseph Jungmann said, "Christ does not offer alone, His people are joined to Him and offer with Him and through Him. Indeed, they are absorbed into Him and form one body with Him by the Holy Spirit who lives in all."

My mother also taught me to pray in the same way for the Holy Souls in purgatory. She told me that this was the perfect opportunity to pray for others too, especially those who have asked me to pray for them. She said that when you hear about people who are suffering all over the world, on the radio, the television, or in the newspaper, you can reach out to them through prayer because prayer is not limited by space and time as we are. The wonderful thing about praying for others in the morning is that they can be included in the prayer that becomes the rest of our day.

St Padre Pio was praying when a lay brother, believing that he was out, burst into his room to find him lost in prayer. The saint dismissed his apologies with the words, "I was just praying for a happy death for my Father."

"But your Father died two years ago!" the brother said, looking rather surprised. Padre Pio looked at him in disbelief and said, "I know he did."

True Christian prayer is not limited to the world of space and time in which we live. It takes us into another dimension where, in the mystical body of Christ, it can reach out now to help those in need, to the four corners of the world, and just as easily to the needy in the past and in the future. That is why the Church made St Thérèse of Lisieux, a young, enclosed Carmelite nun, the patroness of the missions.

Speaking on the radio, a Catholic doctor who was tortured in a Chilean jail said that she received tremendous help from the prayers of friends back home. She likened their prayers to 'waves of love' that sustained her through some of the darkest moments of her ordeal. On the same news program, I heard the story of a group of Christians suffering in Chinese indoctrination camps. They risked their lives to smuggle out a tape recording to their brethren in the West begging for their prayers. Suffering makes people of deep faith sensitive to the extraordinary power of prayer.

3. Reviewing the Day Ahead

The third letter in my blueprint is -R- to remind us that, despite what I have just said, the Morning Offering is not a magic formula. It does not automatically transform the forthcoming day, and that is why something further is required. Spend a few minutes reviewing the day ahead, making a few resolutions that would enable you to try to consecrate every moment of the day to loving God.

It may be by pausing for brief moments of prayer during the day, as Our Lady and the early Christians did, but also in doing humdrum tasks that we keep putting off, like changing the sheets on the beds, putting air into the car tyres, and defrosting the freezer. There is always that friend or relative who is sick or in need whom we should telephone or contact or even visit for a few minutes. We may have to make a resolution to apologise to a family member, a friend, or someone at work for the way we behaved towards them the previous day. It is very difficult to stand up for someone who has been abused by authority at work or elsewhere, or to speak the truth when no one wants to hear it, or to make a stand for what we know is right. But nevertheless, these are some of the more important things that could occupy our minds as part of Morning Prayer.

Chapter 5

A Blueprint for Daily Prayer

St Angela of Foligno, a mother like Mary, said that prayer is the 'School of Divine Love', the place where we learn how to love God. It is here that our loving, or at least our best attempt at loving God, enables Him to love us in return. Love cannot be forced on anyone against their will. This is true of both human and divine love, so unless we try to love God as best we can, His love cannot be forced on us. Forced love is simply a contradiction in terms.

Prayer is the place where we go to keep trying to love God, knowing that God cannot resist loving those who seriously desire to love Him, provided that this desire is genuine. It is proved firstly by the way we make daily time to love Him in prayer, and secondly, by the way we express that love for Him in all we say and do each day. But please remember that at first you will be travelling solely by naked faith because there is little, if any, feeling to support you. Archbishop Fulton Sheen used to say that in human love all the exciting experiences of being in love come at the beginning of the relationship, but with the

Love of God the opposite is true. This has the advantage of keeping bounty hunters at bay while giving true believers the opportunity to show their pure love for God. This is how our true selfless love for God is first shown that makes the infusion of His powerful tangible love possible later, when faith can move mountains.

4. An Act of Faith

The letter -F- can remind us to start by making an act of Faith. I do not mean by reciting some traditional formula of faith, or even professing belief in every article of the creed or in every dogma that the church teaches. There is a time and place for that, but this is the time for something else. Our faith is not firstly a belief in a body of truths, but in a body full of love that was filled to overflowing on the first Easter day.

Ever since the first Pentecost day, God's love has been pouring out of Jesus and into all who freely choose to receive it, drawing us into the fullness of life that is fully embodied in His Risen Body. It is here alone that we are all destined "to live and move and exist" (Acts 17:28), then to experience something of the ecstatic bliss that Jesus experiences now and to all eternity. This is another reason why the fish became a symbol of a Christian in the early Church. They came to see and understand that the love of God was for them what the sea is for the fish,- the living environment outside of which they could not exist. St Augustine takes this analogy one step further, substituting a living sponge for the fish to show that we are not only surrounded at all times by the love of God, but furthermore penetrated through and through by His all-pervading presence. But remember, we do not feel this sublime presence to begin with, for that comes later when our faith has been purified, refined, and capable of experiencing what was before only known by faith alone.

Once all the sublime truths of Christ's continual and abiding presence within us are realised, even without the experience that comes later, then there seems to be only one thing that a person can do. That is to make an act of total abandonment to God.

5. Abandonment to God

The trouble is, we have grown up in a world where nominal or part-time Christians abound, and the truth is, we are probably numbered amongst them. The early Christians had no problem abandoning themselves to God totally, as the man to whom they committed themselves did throughout His life on earth. They knew what was being asked of them from the beginning. While they were under instruction several times a week and praying five times a day, they were seeing the Christians whom they were being prepared to join giving their lives for their belief in Jesus.

Indeed, you would not become a Christian unless you had counted the cost, and that cost may mean losing all your property, all your wealth, and your health, in terrible prison conditions. Here, torture was to be expected and followed by the most hideous forms of death imaginable. In short, no one became a Christian without deciding to abandon their life to God totally, no matter what the cost.

6. Thanksgiving

The next letter, the letter -T-, is a reminder to make an act of thanksgiving to God for all that has been given to us and is continuing to be given to us. It is important to note, however, if we only thank God for what He has done for us, or for what we have managed to get out of Him, then we have not thanked Him as we should. He should be thanked for being God, for being goodness, justice, truth, and beauty. He should be thanked for displaying His own inner glory in the glory of creation that surrounds us, and for the masterpiece of creation, our Risen Lord, in and through whom we are continually being drawn up to share in His own inner life and love, beginning even in this life and then in His everlasting glory in the next.

Take your favourite prayer or hymn of thanksgiving or praise, like the Gloria from the liturgy for instance. Recite it slowly and prayerfully and you will find you are taken out of yourself, out of your world and into God's world where you praise Him, thank Him, and give Him glory with all those who have learned to thank God just for being God. When the full impact of all that God has done for us begins to register in our inmost being, it is time to give Him thanks over and over again for what He continually gives to us. We are all too ready to ask, but sadly all too slow to thank God, not just for what He has done for us personally, but for His goodness, His beauty, and His loving kindness.

The realisation that the All Holy and Utterly Other has chosen to draw us into His own life should bring us physically or at least metaphorically to our knees in adoration. This should naturally overflow into giving praise, glory, and thanksgiving to the One who, though He infinitely transcends us, has chosen to make His home in the very depth of our being. "Make your home in me, as I make mine in you" (John 15:4).

Thanking God for being God leads into the heights of prayer where thanksgiving leads to praise and praise to glorifying God. Ultimately, glorifying God leads to adoration, when we just want to gaze upon Him with a profound reverence and awe that takes us out of ourselves, if only for a time, into brief moments of bliss.

Chapter 6

A Blueprint for Evening Prayer

7. Holy Communion

When you can find a suitable time for evening prayer begin by using the letter –H- for Holy Communion. It reminds us to begin by making a spiritual communion. Perhaps the most holy and all absorbing and spiritually fulfilling moment in the Mass for us, is that sacred moment after we have received Christ into us. It is then that we silently reflect on what "He who is mighty has done for us, and is continually doing".

This moment can be replicated each day at the moment in our daily prayer when we pause, after giving our heartfelt thanks to God, to enjoy what He continually gives us, in what has come to be called a spiritual communion. This is when we come to relish with all our being, the daily bread which is His own body and blood that we ask Him to give us in the Our Father. As for two thousand years or more, daily Mass for the faithful was all but unknown, the daily Bread Christ tells us to pray for, and receive each day, is the indwelling presence of himself, the 'Bread of Life'.

Now is the time to ruminate on and relish the profound mysteries that are at work deep down within us, and to digest and assimilate their sublime meaning and importance for us now and for our future. It is time, too, to allow these truths to percolate through and penetrate our hearts and minds,so we might gaze for as long as possible at the indescribable mysteries that Jesus came to share with us.

8. Examination of Conscience

At the very beginning of every Mass, we start by examining our consciences. We do this so that we can see ever more clearly the sin and selfishness that can alone prevent us from offering ourselves to God with a 'pure and humble heart', and all that can prevent us from receiving His love in return. What happens on the day that we go to celebrate Mass with the whole Catholic community should also happen every day of our lives. For, if we are going to imitate Christ and the way He lived His life, we must endeavour to make every day of our lives into a sacrifice as Jesus Himself did, offering everything that He said and did to His Father and receiving His Father's love in return.

Whilst staying for a brief time at a Cistercian monastery, I met the holiest man I have ever known. He had been in spiritual darkness for many years. Then, one day he became ill and was admitted to the monastery infirmary where he received Holy Communion each day. On three distinct occasions, just as he was about to receive communion, he heard these words, "Only you have been keeping Me out."

We are doing exactly the same, and that is why the letter -E- in the blueprint is to remind us to examine our consciences each day, to pause for a few moments to review our lives since we last prayed. It is time to ask God to show us everything we have done or failed to do that has kept Him out. But most of all, it is time to examine ourselves for the greatest sin of all, the sin of omission, which the Gospel calls the 'Sin Against the Holy Spirit'. In other words, our failure to give some quality space and time each day in which to pray, and most of all to practise the meditation that leads into the prayer where we contemplate our loving Father, in, with, and through Jesus Christ. For without the fruits of this contemplative loving, we will achieve nothing worthwhile or lasting for God.

9. Repentance

After this has been done, it is time to repent by making an Act of formal repentance; that is an act of Contrition for how we have failed in the past. Either a formal act of contrition could be used or perhaps the recitation of what came to be called the 'Jesus Prayer' said several times over, slowly, and prayerfully - "Jesus, son of God, have mercy on me a sinner".

But a sincere expression of personal sorrow in our own words would be better still. Then, we could make a firm purpose of amendment, a genuine decision to try and behave better in the future. Finally, as we become a little more aware of the moral stumbling blocks that trip us up, it is time to try and forestall them. If there is a lazy streak in us, or if we have a hot temper or are prone to making unkind remarks at the expense of others, it is the time to take the necessary steps to avoid falling into these same faults in the forthcoming day and pray for God's help to do what we cannot do without Him.

The sort of daily prayer that Our Lady learnt from her mother, and which was later perfected after her dear son's glorification, was the backbone of her prayer life, as our morning and evening prayer, inspired by and based on hers, should be for us. It will be of particular help when, as we shall see, clouds are gathering in our spiritual journey, and all other forms of prayer seem to be all but impossible. This prayer, taught to many of us by our mothers, like Mary and her son Jesus, can be invaluable most particularly when, as St Teresa of Avila put it, the well runs dry'.

It is important to emphasise that when new converts join the Church because they have had a conversion experience, or what is called in Greek, *Metanoia,* they all too often get ahead of themselves. They immediately take up important roles for which they consider themselves suited. However, the Greek word *Metanoia* means a change of mind whereas the Aramaic word for repentance used by St Peter on the first Pentecost, means an ongoing change of heart and of mind. It is, I am sure, with the best will in the world, that they rush out to use their expertise to change their new home with their new-found fervour, but they would be better advised to follow the example of St Paul. They should rather rush out into the desert for some years, to learn and practise the prayers, the meditation, and the contemplation that will alone equip them to do what St Paul did. Here they should be first grounded in the same sort of daily prayer that Our Lady herself practised before and after her son's glorification. Then, when the 'well does run dry', as it will, there will be a daily pattern of prayer on which to fall back on to prevent them from going astray.

Part 2 Meditation

Chapter 7

A New Form of Prayer

While continuing with the daily prayer that we use in imitation of Christ, it is time to come to know and to love God. The place where we must look to seek his love is in the person of Jesus Christ Our Lord. Before the first Pentecost, Our Lady, the apostles, and the disciples had come to know and love Our Lord as the perfect human being to whom Mary gave birth. They prayed with Him, alongside Him, and together with Him as best they could. However, on the first Pentecost day something dramatic happened that would change the way they prayed, and for that matter, change the whole context and direction of their spiritual lives and their way of evangelising others. When they received the Holy Spirit, they were drawn up by Him into the Risen and Glorified Christ. They were drawn up into His mystical body so that now, unlike the past, they would not just pray with or alongside Him, but actually within Him.

For the Apostles, this new prayer would not be so immediately dramatic as it was for Our Lady because they were still sinners, and their

42

sins prevented them from being as closely united with Christ as she was. It was these sins that prevented them from experiencing the profound contemplative prayer that would enthral them after several years of further spiritual and ascetical formation in Jerusalem. Then, fully united with Christ their Risen Lord, and so with his contemplation of his Father, they received the fruits of contemplation that would enable them to become other Christs and say, "I live now not with my own life, but with the life of Christ who lives in me" (Galatians 2:20), as the apostle St Paul put it. Then, as Christ promised at the Last Supper, they would be able to do all that Christ himself did whilst He was on earth, and in the words of Christ Himself, even greater things. However, although it would take them years to come to experience true contemplation, because Our Lady was immaculately conceived and therefore free from sin, the very moment that she received the Holy Spirit, she was not just taken up and into her beloved son, but when she prayed she was taken up into His prayer, into His loving contemplation of the Father to further receive the fruits of Contemplation for herself, and for all those whom Christ had asked her to become a mother.

The only way to come to know and love God, as He is in Himself, is to begin where Our Lady herself began; by coming to love Him as he was made flesh and blood in the person of her son Jesus Christ. That is why Our Lady became such an important person in the early Church, when according to tradition, she settled down with her new foster son, St John. In order that new converts could come to know Jesus as she and the other apostles and first disciples had known Him, meditation became paramount as the gateway to contemplation. This prayer would enable those who had not known Christ, to pore over every detail of His life on earth, reflecting and ruminating on it, and so come to know and love Him.

They were taught to do this in such a way that their love for Jesus would not just impel them to become closer to Him and copy Him, but to be united with Him. Our Lady's contribution to this new form of prayer called meditation was unique. Who else was there when she first learnt that she was to conceive the son of God? Who else was there at his birth to tell of the moment when the infinite God became a helpless child to be laid in a manger? Who else was alive to tell of the flight into Egypt, the presentation in the Temple, and the hidden years when she was intimately involved in helping the Christ child to grow in stature and in divine wisdom as he prepared for his public ministry? Who was more painfully there when he was so cruelly put to death and humiliated as a slave or as a common criminal?

That is why in the early Church and in the present Church there is no one else who so relentlessly calls upon her children to meditate on Christ's life and most particularly on his Passion and death in order to come to love him. Only this love generated by loving Him as he once was on earth, can be transformed into a love that wants to be united with Him now as He is in heaven.

This new form of meditation that led on and into Contemplation, was first practised by lay-people for hundreds of years before monks or religious were even thought of. Like the Jewish spirituality from which it emerged, Christianity began in the home where it was first learnt and practised by mothers and fathers and brothers and sisters. If like Christ Himself, or His apostles, family members sought time outside the home for more intense moments of prayer in solitude, they nevertheless returned to their homes. But make no mistake about it, the initial prayers they were taught, be it different forms of vocal or liturgical prayer or the new form of meditation, would lead to mystical contemplation, as can be seen in the experience of St Paul (2 Corinthians 12:1-7).

The only way to God was in, with, and through Christ. But not just in Him as an inanimate object, but as a loving human being. When Christ contemplates He is caught up in an act of mutual loving in which His love rises to God and God's love descends into Him. This mutual loving is the Holy Spirit. So, when our prayer life leads us on into Christ and into His contemplation, which it must else we will never be united with God, something utterly sublime takes place. We are actually led, at least in some measure, into the life of the Three in One. This is both the ultimate intuition and experience of the great saints and mystics and is the sign of their orthodoxy.

The profound mystical spirituality that was generated and lived in the early Church is not measured by whether or not you find them using the sort of mystical language and terminology that took centuries to find its way into Christian literature. It is measured by the simple principle first enunciated by Christ Himself as I keep insisting: "It will be by their fruits that you will know them". These fruits, detailed by St Thomas Aquinas and called the fruits of contemplation, are freely given to us when our contemplation is one with Christ's own contemplation. For when we are one with Him in His contemplation, then we are one with Him in our action.

Chapter 8

The Rise and Demise of Meditation

The role of Our Lady in the first decades of early Christianity cannot be exaggerated. That God left her on earth to be our Mother was so that she should teach the first Christians by both word and example how to develop their prayer lives. She did this in such a way that, in her Son Jesus Christ, they could be united with God the Father who had created them to enjoy eternal life with Him in the next life. She did not just want to guide people through meditation into contemplation so that they could enjoy sublime otherworldly experiences of God's love, but something much more. She wanted them to receive the fruits of Contemplation as both she and her son had done. For without these supernatural gifts, her son would not be able to continue his redemptive work through them as intended.

Both she, the apostles, and the first disciples therefore taught newcomers how to come to know and love Jesus, as they did whilst He was on earth. It was for this reason that they introduced a new form of prayer called meditation. This practice was encouraged at four specific times. At nine o'clock in the morning, they were told to meditate on Christ's condemnation to death, the scourging at the pillar, and the crowning with thorns. At midday, they were to meditate on His crucifixion and the sufferings that He had to endure as He was being nailed to the Cross. At three o'clock in the afternoon, they were to meditate on his death and the gruelling agonising moments that preceded his final act of Love. Christians were also encouraged to rise at midnight to meditate on the Resurrection. This of course might seem too much to ask of modern Catholics, but remember before electric lights, people tended to go to bed much earlier than we do and rise much earlier too. For ancient people the evening was the time to tell stories at the fireside. With no distractions from the Mass Media, ordinary people developed prodigious memories. Some Jews, for instance, knew almost all the Bible by heart just as some Greeks came to know the Iliad and the Odyssey by heart.

For the early Christians, these evening get-togethers were the times when those who had known Christ personally heard endless stories about His life, death, and Resurrection and committed them to memory. At the weekly Mass, sometimes two or three Apostles or disciples would electrify their congregation telling stories of all that Christ said and did. But notice, when it specifically came to teaching their followers how to meditate, it was not on Christ's life in general that they were taught to reflect, but on the most perfect act of Love ever enacted, when he gave His life for us on the Cross. Speaking many centuries later, St Bonaventure said, "I beg you to meditate on the Passion and death of Christ". Yet again, I beg you to meditate on His passion and death. As I have described in my talks on prayer and in my books, it was while meditating for weeks on the passion and death of Christ that I was led on into contemplation.

I know the times set aside for this practice in the early Church would not be convenient to modern Catholics, but if they would travel further on this road to perfection they simply must find time for meditation. If you cannot find time to meditate on the love of God, then what is time for. Statisticians tell us that we spend many hours every week, if not every day, glued to the Mass Media in one form or another to please ourselves. Can we not spend a fraction of that time trying to learn how to love the God who can radically transform our lives for the better, when the Mass Media does the opposite? That is precisely what happened in the early Church when Christians were not only personally changed through the Meditation that leads to contemplation, but so were others and on a grand scale. What other power than the power of God's Love working through simple, ordinary Christians could change a massive pagan empire into a Christian Empire in such a short time? It was the God-given love that is generated in contemplation that worked such a miracle, but without the meditation that first taught Christians how to respond to the love of God in Jesus Christ, such a sublime form of prayer would be utterly unattainable.

For over three hundred years all was well, and it was hoped that what Christianity did for the Roman world would be done for the rest of the world. However, disaster struck when a heresy called Arianism crept into Catholic spirituality like a cancer to corrode and corrupt it from within. It is generally known that ninety percent of Catholics succumbed to this heresy that insisted that Christ was not God, but merely a mortal. That this heresy was an affront to God, His Son, and to the long held dogmatic teaching of the Church is well known. However, what is not known is that this heresy all but completely destroyed the profound contemplative teaching and practice of the early Church. If Christ was not God then no amount of meditation on His purely human loving could lead onward into His divine contemplation. The sublime spirituality that had been the vital living principle that made God's new people radio-active with divine loving was simply destroyed from the inside.

Meditation was further undermined in the Eastern Church when Iconoclasm taught that all religious images should be destroyed including images in the mind. In the early Church, it was lay apostles working out of family life who evangelised the world. In the Dark Ages it was left to monks working out of monasteries who tried to fill the gap. But the number simply did not add up, and so the Church had to sail on, until at the end of the Dark Ages, a Christian renaissance turned the clock back. Serious crimes against Christians in the Holy Land finally impelled Pope Urban II to announce a crusade in 1095. Once again, the Holy Land was opened to pilgrims and a new Catholic revival ensued.

Pilgrims returned full of exciting stories of how they saw where Christ was born, where He grew up, where He preached, where He lived, where He died, and from where He rose again from the dead. St Bernard of Clairvaux developed a new theology centred on Christ. What he did for academics, St Francis of Assisi, who visited the Holy Land himself, did for ordinary people. With the return to meditation, contemplation followed, and in the next six centuries or more, the Catholic Church produced the greatest crop of writers detailing the contemplative life ever known in its history.

Sadly, just as the heresy of Arianism had taken away contemplative spirituality before, Quietism, a new heresy, took it away once more at the end of the seventeenth century. This heresy insisted that to practise contemplative prayer, and perhaps attain what St Teresa of Avila called the 'Prayer of Quiet', we should simply do nothing but wait on God. Molinos, Quietism's founder, was not only leading people back into Protestantism, but into serious sin. He told his followers to do nothing about temptations, for only God could take them away. At his trial he and his followers were convicted of myriad serious sexual sins, clear evidence of his teachings.

The effect and influence of the anti-mystical witch-hunts that followed in the wake of Quietism have continued down to the present day. Despite this, the real danger and damage done by Quietism, unlike Arianism, is the fact that hardly anyone has ever heard of this heresy. The vast majority of the faithful, and that includes priests, religious, and theologians, do not even know that, thanks to the age-old reaction to Quietism, they have been living in a Catholic world that is bereft. It is bereft of the vital infused love that animated the first Christian communities and they are not even aware of it.

If it was by the fruits of contemplation that the Church first converted the ancient world, it has been by the demise of those same fruits that the Church has scandalised the modern world. For without infused love given through contemplation, Catholics do not have the inner spiritual strength that vitalised their first ancestors. Just as it was once the laity who were the means of converting the ancient world, it is they who are once again being called upon to convert the modern world, beginning with themselves.

Chapter 9

The Practice of Meditation

The practical teaching of our first Catholic forebears is clear. If we would love God we must first find His love, as it is made flesh and blood in Jesus Christ Our Lord. Meditating on His love for us should primarily be centred on those passages from the sacred scripture that manifest most clearly the love of the most lovable man who ever lived. And most particularly on the most perfect act of love that Christ ever performed at the end of His life. Perhaps, I can best show how to begin Meditation from scratch by telling you how I managed to get started.

My search did not begin because I was a pious youth but a needy one. In an age when dyslexia was not understood, I thought God might help me and I turned to prayer. When I turned to the school spiritual director for help, he told me that if I wanted to come to know and love God I must first begin by coming to know and love Him in Jesus Christ. This he said would lead me on to union with Him and through Him with God His Father. This caused a certain

51

confusion in me at the time. Only six weeks earlier I had fallen in love for the first time, and loving God as I loved my girlfriend just did not seem to add up. So I put it to my spiritual director. He was very understanding. He explained how in the Old Testament God was sometimes called a Mother as well as a Father, endowed with feminine as well as male characteristics. He showed how some of the Fathers of the Church spoke of what they called the *anima* and the *animus* in God. In other words, God is neither male nor female, but the qualities of maleness and femaleness can be found uniquely balanced and brought to perfection in Him and perfectly expressed in His love for all that He created. These same qualities must therefore be found in Jesus Christ, in whom the fullness of the Father's love is to be found here on earth. That is why in responding to His love, men and women can respond equally, yet differently, and both ultimately find their completion in Him.

Thanks to the school spiritual director, what I had originally thought impossible suddenly became possible, and the ambiguity about trying to love Jesus no longer held me back. I decided to study Him more and more deeply so that I could come to love Him, and in loving Him come to experience the only love that could change me permanently for the better, leading me onward to the perfection that I desired more than anything else.

Long before television, I became addicted to the radio, or the wireless as we called it then. My favourite programme for children was called, 'How things began'. It featured Uncle Jim who would take young listeners with him back into the past to see and experience for ourselves how the world was created, and how the past still influences the world we live in. He used to say, "Open your eyes and see, open your ears and hear, open your noses and smell. You must so immerse yourself in the past so that it becomes as the present. Then, use your minds to understand what you see and you will be able to make history real in a way that you will be able to apprehend it like never before".

Thanks to Uncle Jim, when the principle and purpose of meditation was explained to me, I was able to go back into the past as he taught me. This time my goal was not to see and understand the beginnings of the physical world, but to see and understand the beginnings of the Christian world. I was there when Christ was born. I saw it with my own inner eyes. I heard what was being said by Mary and Joseph, what the shepherds and the three kings had to say, why they suddenly had to make a dash for Egypt to live in exile until Herod was dead. I visited Nazareth when Jesus was growing up, but most importantly of all, I was there when He was baptised in the river Jordan. I followed Him throughout His life on earth listening to what He had to say and watching how people reacted to Him, especially when out of unprecedented care and compassion He healed the sick and the dying and even raised the dead.

It was about Easter time when meditation came to a climax. Throughout Lent I had been beguiled by the profound mystical teaching of Jesus during the Last Supper. Then, after I heard and assimilated what He said as I imagined myself sitting with Him at the same table as the Apostles, all my inner faculties were raised to a state of high emotional intensity. It was not just that He said He wanted us to be His friends, but even more than that. He wanted us to be united with Him in such a way that He could make His home in us and we could make our home in Him. So, with Him all things would become possible, even the impossible, as I had been able to visualise Him performing the impossible throughout His time on earth. But what finally moved me more than anything else was how the world He had come to teach how to love simply rejected Him. They not only rejected Him, but they hated Him for it. When my meditation followed Him from the Upper Room and into the Garden of Gethsemane, I saw for myself as I prayed with the Apostles the terrible toll that His approaching passion and death was having upon Him.

Unlike the Apostles, I knew what was coming next. What made Him sweat to blood was not just what He would have to endure, but what little effect it would have on the world for which He was prepared to give His all, and in such an appalling way. It was perhaps not so much hatred for what He represented that added to His suffering, but apathy and indifference. I vowed that I would not desert Him, and using all the inner human resources that were available to me - my memory, imagination, and mind with its powers of reasoning and understanding - I tried to remain faithful. I was there in spirit, in mind, and in heart amongst the soldiers with the bystanders as Jesus was first scourged, crowned with thorns, and then ridiculed by drunken louts. I followed in my mind and in my imagination over many weeks as He carried His cross all the way to Calvary and I was there too when in all but pitch darkness He was taken down from the Cross and laid in the sepulchre.

It was at this point that my human love for the love of God in Jesus Christ reached its climax as I meditated on His Resurrection and reflected on all that had led up to this dramatic, otherworldly conclusion. All I wanted to do day after day was to gaze upon Him now in His risen glory. All I wanted to do was to gaze upon Him without any words. All had been said, all had been seen; all had been reflected upon. All I wanted to do was to gaze in a profound contemplative stillness on the One who had done so much, not just for the world in general, but for me in particular.

Chapter 10

From Meditation to Contemplation

Let me summarise the practical steps to take in order to learn how to practise the meditation that leads to contemplation. First of all, pick up the Gospels and make them your spiritual reading a little at a time, day by day. However, when it comes to the time that you have set aside in which to practise meditation, go to the discourse at the Last Supper in St John's Gospel and read it slowly and prayerfully, endlessly pausing to allow the powerful and all-pervading words of Christ to penetrate deep down into the very marrow of your being. Then, gradually over the weeks, or even months, move on and into meditating on the Passion and Death of Christ in all the Gospel accounts. This will enable you to see and contrast the most sublime loving teacher who has ever walked on this earth, with the evil that He came to supplant, embodied in men who hated and wanted to destroy Him in the most cruel and despicable way conceivable.

In order to make your meditation methodical, use what I call the four 'R's: Read, Reflect, React, and then Rest. Read the text as you would read good poetry, poring over every word, reading again several times over depending on the profundity of the text. Then, reflect on what you have read. Ruminate on it as St Augustine would say, asking the Holy Spirit who inspired these words to inspire you to understand them ever more deeply. Then, react to what you have been meditating on in prayer, as you express your feelings to God in your own words. In time, as the full impact of what you have been reading and reflecting upon begins to take hold of your mind, your heart, and your feelings, just remain still to savour the sacred text. In time, all you will want to do is to be still to digest and then rejoice in what you have just read.

When I first arrived at this state of inner repose, or what has been called 'Acquired Contemplation' at the height of meditation, my pride misinterpreted what I was experiencing. Like so many others, I thought that I had arrived at the heights of the mystic way. But I had to think again when suddenly the sweet, all-absorbing prayer that enveloped me suddenly came to an abrupt end never to return again, at least in quite the same way.

Although I did not know it at the time, God had heard the prayer that I had been making and answered it by leading me into true mystical contemplation, though it initially felt more like purgatory on earth than anything else. At least that is what I thought at the time, and I was right! The point that I want to make is that perseverance in meditation enables a person to come to know and love God as He was embodied over two thousand years ago in Jesus Christ. This is terribly important. That is why you cannot bypass meditation as some have tried to do, throwing themselves into obscure states of transcendental awareness or repeating mantras to experience peaceful states of mind. They are deceiving themselves into believing that their self-induced feelings of inner peace are equivalent to what

Christian mystics call the 'Prayer of the Quiet' or 'Full Union'. But when ignorance is bliss, it is folly to be wise as I have found out for myself.

Coming to know and love Christ through meditation is the beginning of true Christian wisdom: it cannot be bypassed for the latest fads. The whole point of this prayer, which was elemental to the first Christians, was that in it you not only came to know and love Christ, as those who came to know and love Him whilst He was on earth, but in so doing, you have clearly manifested to God that you genuinely want to love Him by the sacrifices you have made by giving quality space and time to this end. Your desire to love Christ and to be united with Him, a desire that comes to fever pitch in what has been called 'Acquired Contemplation' has been proven by your perseverance. But there is a problem. Although it is possible to come to know and even love someone long since dead, you cannot possibly be united with them. That is why, to answer your unspoken prayer, the Holy Spirit draws you out of meditating on Christ, as He once was, to meditating Him as He is now, Risen and glorified.

The word for this new form of meditation is Contemplation. Whereas meditation could be learnt and practised by us, contemplation is a pure gift from God. When God gives this gift, it so captivates our heart's desire, that our will is enthralled by the strange new experience of the love of God. Although our will does not tangibly experience God's love initially, the pull towards God's love is such that the meditation we thought we had just mastered suddenly comes to an abrupt end. It is now Contemplation that galvanises the will, drawing it to the union that it desires with such power that it cannot be marshalled to practise meditation any longer. The meditation that has led a person on so far will never be possible in quite the same way again. The only way forward is to follow the strange pull towards God that is experienced both inside and outside of prayer. This strange pull, seemingly leading nowhere but into a new type of obscure form of prayer where distractions and temptations seem to reign supreme, puzzles the new contemplatives and makes them think that they must be on the wrong path. The greatest temptation of all is to pack up this futile form of prayer and, if meditation is impossible, at least spend their time doing something useful.

Interestingly enough, St John of the Cross said that this strange new desire for God is one of the signs that the Holy Spirit has led a person out of meditation and into contemplation. Although they may think that Christ has gone from their spiritual lives, they are wrong, because now the Holy Spirit has taken them more deeply up and into Christ, into the beginning of a union with Him that leads to union with God, in, with and through Him.

Part 3 Contemplation

Chapter 11

Contemplation - A Pure Gift of God

One of the most poignant passages from the whole of spiritual literature comes from St Augustine. In his Confessions he writes, "You have made us for yourself O Lord and our heart is restless until it rests in you". The reason why this profound passage touches so many hearts, whether they be religious or non-religious, is because, deep down in the very nether regions of our personalities, deeper even than the irrational forces for evil that too often shame us, there is a yearning for love without measure. This yearning will never be satisfied until it can be enveloped by the cornucopia of infinite love that finds its perfection in God. When we read in the scriptures that we are made in the image and likeness of God, it does not mean so much the image and likeness of the God who dwells in light inaccessible, but rather in the image and likeness of the God who was made flesh and blood in Jesus Christ to show us the way back to the place where the perfection of all love can be found.

It was in Him, Christ the King, that all things were created in the first place, and through the goodness of God that He was born into a world of matter and form, of flesh and blood, of unredeemed chaos, so that He could show us the way back to the person in whom our heart's deepest desire for perfect love can alone be satisfied.

Through our daily prayer we may have tried to imitate the way Christ prayed as He was taught to pray by his mother over two thousand years ago. Then something happened. Perhaps it was a book we read, a retreat we attended, a person we met, or some sort of personal encounter with God that made us pause and think. It made us decide to become something more than just nominal Sunday morning Catholics. We wanted to enter more deeply into the faith that we had taken far too easily for granted. It was then that the deep desire for the love of God led us to seek out that love as it is so perfectly embodied in the person of Jesus Christ. So in Meditation we learnt to come to know and love Him, as the First Christians came to know and love Him before us. The deep desire for God that made our hearts restless to rest in Him from the very beginning found a new fulfilment that it had never known in the same way before. It was our free choice, the choice of our free will. Despite the sacrifices that we initially had to make to find quality space and time for meditation, we never regretted it. Then after many months, or even several years of fidelity to meditation, something suddenly happened to change our whole prayer life and the whole of our spiritual life forever. The first major change came because we decided that it was time to better our spiritual life in order to come to know and love God more perfectly in Jesus Christ. Then, and quite out of the blue, God decided, because of our fidelity and the seriousness of our intent that we have proved through both words and actions, to lead us onwards into a deeper form of prayer called Contemplation.

Meditation began because it was our choice. Contemplation begins

61

because it is God's choice. That is why it has been the teaching of the Catholic Church from the beginning that Contemplation is a pure gift of God. However, for the believer it does not seem like a gift at the beginning, for once God takes hold of our free will and begins to draw it to Himself, it can no longer operate as before. This means that meditation comes to an abrupt halt because our own free will is so drawn to God that it loses its power to control the operations of the mind, the imagination, and of the memory, at least in prayer. All our restless heart wants to do now when it comes to the prayer time that it had previously given so religiously to meditation, is to gaze upon God's Love. Jesus Christ however has not gone away; far from it. Meditation has meant that we have so developed and deepened our love for Him that we have become more at one with Him than ever before. Thanks to this love that has been generated in Him, we are yearning incessantly for the God who created us, and for the destiny for which He created us in the first place.

We are now in Christ, within not just his mystical body, but together with Him in His loving contemplation of God our Father. However, truth to tell, and this is the bad news, although the desire for God is still there and has in fact been strengthened in meditation, it is still comparatively weak and when we go to pray we are tantalised by a thousand and one distractions that pick and paw at the mind from the inside. It makes the believer yearn for the halcyon days of Acquired Contemplation, as the Israelites once yearned in their desert for the 'fleshpots of Egypt'. That is why spiritual writers from the beginning have called this new development in prayer, the Desert, the Wilderness, the Prayer of Faith, the House of Self-knowledge, the Cloud of Unknowing, or the Dark Night of the Soul.

In the past, before Quietism took mystical prayer and contemplative spirituality out of true Catholic Spirituality, the mystic way was well charted for all to see. There was an abundance of spiritual directors who knew the way, not just from books, but from personal experience. In those days, novice masters and novice mistresses saw the whole point and purpose of the Noviciate as the time and place to lead their charges on, into, and through Meditation and into Contemplation before first vows were taken. The religious life and the seminary were the places where spiritual directors were formed to lead the laity onward and into the profound contemplative Spirituality that first thrived amongst themselves in the early Church. But sadly now that has all gone. It must however return, or we are lost, for without God and His love we have no power to do anything. And be sure that the contemplative prayer, that is for all, is the only place where that love is received in abundance. And that love is nothing other than the fullness of God's love that gives to the receiver all the infused virtues and all the fruits and gifts of the Holy Spirit, without which they would be spiritually bankrupt. We have sadly seen the consequences of this spiritual bankruptcy in recent years.

At the outset of what has been called the Mystic Way, or the beginning of Contemplative prayer, all seems lost to the traveller. If this is the way to perfection they surmise, I would rather look for another way or just give up what seems to have become impossible. Surely, I could be far better employed getting out into the world and doing some good rather than locking myself up in a barren prayer life and going round in circles doing nothing. That is why in this strange new world, prayer has been called 'the prayer of nothing' or even the 'prayer of incompetence' because nothing seems to be happening, and you feel totally incompetent to do anything. Later, with hindsight, the traveller will come to realise and understand that the whole point of this prayer is that your pride learns that of itself it can do nothing, and that you are quite incompetent at doing the good that you thought you were doing before. The French mystic Père

Lallemant said that you can do more in a month with contemplation than in a lifetime without it.

That the vast majority of those who have come so far simply give up, not just prayer, but the spiritual life and even the faith, is sadly a fact. It is a fact that, as St John of the Cross insists, is due to ignorance more than anything else. Let me therefore arm you with the truth and encourage you to abandon yourself ever more completely to God's Holy Spirit, so that He can be your guide, for the Spiritual directors who were once to be found in abundance are, for the reasons that I have detailed, thin on the ground.

Chapter 12

Learning Divine Loving

As I said earlier, St Angela of Foligno said that prayer is the *Scola Divini Amoris* or the School of Divine Love. In other words, the place where we go to learn how to love God. However, there is another meaning of this name for prayer that is too often missed. Let me explain. It is not only the place where we go to learn to love God, but the place that we go to learn Divine Loving. In other words, we learn the same sort and quality of loving with which God loved His people in the Old Testament, and the same sort and quality of loving with which He loved people in the New Testament, through His son Our Lord Jesus Christ. In short, we must learn a pure, selfless, and totally unconditional love that has never before been seen on earth. Now, here is the point for the person who seeks the perfection that can only be attained through union with God. The only way we can attain union with God is by learning and practising, in the School of Divine Love, the selfless unconditional loving that can alone unite us, firstly with Christ, and then in, with, and through Him with the Father.

Once this is realised then the strange new world in which people find themselves after meditation makes total sense, even from a human point of view. God has led them into this new predicament so that they can now learn through practice the selfless, unconditional loving that can alone unite them with God. Let me now give you the practical steps that you must take to journey on ever more deeply into 'mystical contemplation'. And be sure of this, you will have to journey on for many months, if not for years, practising giving without receiving, before you have any clear and certain intimation of God's presence. Nor will God ever make His presence apparent as long as you keep looking at your watch and asking, 'When am I going to experience 'The Prayer of Quiet', 'The Prayer of Full Union'? When am I going to have a Rapture or an Ecstasy? How long before the Mystical Marriage? The whole point and purpose of this journey is that you learn to become a selfless, unconditional lover like the God who created you, else union of any sort, never mind the sort that leads to mystical experience, will be quite impossible.

How do you proceed from where you are at the beginning of the mystic way? Firstly, in order to demonstrate by your very presence that you are in earnest, give exactly the same time for this dark, obscure contemplation as you did when meditation was at its height. The reason contemplation is always dark to begin with is because, as it first enters into you, the light of God's love first highlights all the sin and selfishness that resides in you, and which therefore, prevents you from residing in God. The darkness does not come from God but from yourself. You are now in what St Catherine of Siena called 'The House of Self Knowledge', where God's love will enable you to see what has been keeping Him out and what will continue to keep Him out unless, after seeing your sinfulness, you take action. You must take action by accepting it, confessing it, and then continuing on your journey, for you will never be able to experience the love of

God until you have been sufficiently purified and refined in the Dark Night of the Soul. Next, how do you pray in this dark and testing spiritual desert? Because the truth is that although you have always had temptations and distractions in prayer, you will never have had them so strong and so powerful as they become in The Dark Night of the Soul. Now, St Teresa of Avila said that you will not just virtually always have distractions and temptations in prayer, but that you cannot actually pray without them. Why? Because every time that you turn away from them, you are making an act of love. You are saying no to the world from which they have come and yes to the God who dwells in the world to which you want to go; No to self-love, yes to the love of God. In short, you are making acts of love, and it is only by practising acts of love that a habit of love is gradually formed generating an inner disposition or attitude of heart and mind. So, if you have fifty distractions in fifteen minutes, you have practised selflessness fifty times. On the other hand, if you have only had one or two distractions that occupy the whole of the time in which you should have been learning how to love God, then that is of course a waste of time because you have simply been daydreaming, usually about future pleasure seeking.

As contemplation begins because God Himself takes the initiative by drawing your free will towards himself, you will find it impossible to meditate as before. In the overall journey of the Spiritual life, meditation would usually only take up a small percentage of your prayer time, the major part being taken up in contemplation, first in darkness, then for those who persevere, in light. So many people have found their own way into the contemplative way without even noticing it, for instance through saying and meditating on the Rosary. But without the help of a director who knows the way ahead, not just out of books but out of experience, they can spend years doing the spiritual equivalent of the Hokey Pokey or the 'Hokey Cokey' as it is called in Britain. St Teresa of Avila used to say that she would rather have no spiritual director than a bad one. So as good ones are so rare today for the reasons that I have already explained, let me encourage you to press on using the prayer of the heart, as I will explain shortly.

Chapter 13

The Prayer of the Heart

What I am writing now is the most important message in this book, or for that matter, in any of the books that I have ever written. Please give your full attention to what follows, for your whole spiritual life depends on it, not just in this life but in the next life too.

It is the result of over sixty-five years of trying to journey myself in the mystic way, in which contemplation is the daily prayer to which a person is called when they go to prayer. Without this prayer, I could not have given a fifteen-part course on prayer, nor written over a dozen books on the subject. The mystic way begins and contemplation commences, not when we choose but when we have shown, usually in meditation, that we not only want to keep loving God, but that we want to be united with Him. The perseverance that we have shown in previous prayer is crucial, for it demonstrates to God the serious resolve that we have for the union that only He can give. It is then that God does but one thing. Through His Holy Spirit, He draws us more powerfully than before towards Himself to prepare us for the union for which He has created us, and for which we have been yearning, as St Augustine said, from the very beginning of our human existence.

What we immediately experienced when God takes this initiative, however, is quite other than we might have expected. Because it begins when He draws our free will towards Himself, our free will loses the power that it had before to direct and order our minds, our imaginations, and our memories in order to meditate. Meditation enabled us to discover God's Love as it was embodied in the human person of Jesus, as He lived and died for us two thousand years ago. However, as we cannot be united with someone who lived so long ago in the past, the Holy Spirit has been sent to draw us up and into Him, as He is alive and living in the present in His Risen, Glorified, Mystical Body, so that in, with, and through Him we are able to contemplate the Father. Without the sensible and often even emotional experiences that we once enjoyed in meditation, this new form of prayer seems to be comparatively dark and barren and filled more intensively than ever with distractions and temptations. And, despite a strong yearning for God, there are none of the human satisfactions and spiritual pleasures that we experienced before.

The greatest of all the temptations to which, through ignorance, the majority succumb is to run away from this strange new world in which we find ourselves. Those who persevere come what may have to take up their daily cross to follow Christ within this new form of prayer. The very nature of the cross that they are called upon to carry, consists in daily trying to practise the pure, selfless unconditional loving that Christ Himself practised every day of His life on earth.

The essential nature of this cross consists in making repeated acts of love, despite the continual distractions and temptations and unaccompanied by the sort of satisfaction and sensible feelings that was experienced before. In short, they are practising divine loving, the divine loving with which God loved his people, firstly in the Old Testament, and secondly in the New Testament, in and through His son Jesus Christ. This is the only way that divine loving is learnt, the divine loving that can alone unite us with Jesus Christ, and then in, with, and through Him, with His Father in whom we are called to reside to all eternity.

All these profound thoughts are, however, far away from the minds of beginners in the mystic way when they are for the first time called to contemplation. In order to help their desire for God to remain fixed upon Him, the Catholic mystical tradition teaches the practice of what came to be called 'The Prayer of the Heart'. It should ideally be a brief prayer of your own choosing, if not of your own making, that is redolent with the truth of your present relationship with God. This is no place for false or phoney prayers that you think you ought to use, or what you think God would like to hear. Now, although you may not realise it, you are in Christ the New Temple, and with Him practising the 'New Worship in Spirit' and in Truth. That is why your prayer must be simple and truthful, because through it you are offering yourself to God while simultaneously asking Him to help you in your need.

The sort of prayer that you may use or choose should be something like, 'O God come to my aid, O Lord make haste to help me'. Or you could use the Jesus prayer. or simply 'Your will be done'. The prayer should be repeated over and over again to help you to do two things simultaneously, namely to keep your heart's desire remain fixed on God, while trying to suffocate the temptations and distractions that would draw you away from your purpose. In time, the full phrase or sentence may be too much, and you will instinctively know when to reduce it to an even shorter prayer like, 'O God come to my aid', 'Jesus help' or 'Jesus mercy, Mary help', or simply the Holy Name itself. The short prayers I have given are only examples to make my point. It is far better for you to choose prayers for yourself because they must embody how you genuinely feel and how you relate to God at this testing point in the spiritual life.

Eventually when you begin to experience the presence of God, your prayer will change accordingly. It may be, 'My Lord and my God', the spontaneous prayer of St Thomas when Christ appeared to Him in the Upper Room, or 'My God and my All', the prayer that St Francis used when he experienced the love of God, now the motto of the Franciscan Order in its Latin form, *Deus Meus et Omnia*. Eventually, the more powerful God's presence becomes, all a person wants to do is to remain silent as the all-invasive love of God enthrals them.

Chapter 14

Perseverance in Divine Loving

Whatever happens in this strange new form of prayer, where divine, selfless sacrificial loving is learnt, keep giving the same time for prayer. Give the same time for prayer in darkness and gloom that you gave when all seemed to be sweetness and light. Simply persevere come what may, in good times, and in bad times. This is the only way that you can learn to love as God loves, the same sort of love that we see embodied in Christ when He was on earth. If we are not prepared to learn this sort of love. then we cannot be united with God. Despite your best efforts, you will run away and look elsewhere for what you can in fact only find in prayer. When this happens, start again immediately no matter what you think or feel, for this is the only way forward.

You will not only falter and fall within prayer, but you will do likewise outside of prayer too. Sin will not only become an embarrassment to you, but it can lead you away, not only from contemplative prayer, but from living a decent moral life too. The watchword must be, as the saints continually insisted, get up immediately without delay. It is not the Pride before a fall that is so much the problem in the spiritual life, but the pride after the fall, for it makes a person so ashamed that they run away and hide from God as Adam did in the Garden of Eden. The moment you fall must be the moment you get up so that no time is wasted thanks to your pride. Get up immediately, St Francis of Assisi insisted, make an act of contrition, go to confession, and begin again without delay. Add up the time in your life that pride has made you run away and hide from God, and you will see the time wasted that could otherwise have made you into the saint that God originally intended. When you stop falling you will be in Heaven, but when you stop getting up you will be in Hell. Remember, the difference between us and the saints is not that we sin and they did not, but that they finally learnt the humility that enabled them to keep getting up immediately when we do not.

As the months or the years pass by, the prayers of the heart become like the oars on a rowing boat as you travel downstream towards the sea. When the boat is set on its course and is travelling smoothly forward, then you can rest awhile enjoying the scenery as the boat proceeds silently towards its destiny. Then, if the boat slows down or begins to veer towards the bank, you once more need to use the oars to set it back on course. Eventually, as the tidal current begins to draw you onwards, you need the oars less and less. Then, when you find yourself at sea, you can raise the sails and allow the wind of God's Holy Spirit to guide you to your destiny with little need to use your oars. At the beginning of your journey, you are very active, but the more God takes control you become more passive.

The first time that you receive any intimation that God is in this strange new form of prayer is when you gradually begin to realise that without it you are somehow spiritually diminished. Then, after several more months of perseverance you become aware of a subtle form of presence. It is hardly detectable at first, but it becomes more detectable as you continue to persevere in the darkness using 'The Prayer of the Heart'. As this subtle sense of awareness grows, it begins to feel like the sense of presence, described for instance by the romantic poets, except that it is not inspired by some moving scenery, some artistic masterpiece, or some piece of beautiful music. It is inspired by the Maker of them all.

Eventually, if you continue to persevere, not because you are a bounty hunter seeking sublime spiritual experiences for yourself but for the love of God, whether He gives you tangible experiences of His presence or not, then a more dramatic departure takes place in your prayer life. The same subtle experience that you have already experienced, suddenly and without warning, lifts you up and absorbs you into the presence of God. This is what St Teresa of Avila called the 'Prayer of Quiet'. Then, and without any further warning, this same experience instantly becomes so intense that it raises you up within yourself to such a degree that you no longer have any distractions at all. St Teresa of Avila calls this 'Full Union'. If you had ever doubted the existence of God before, then henceforth you can be sure you will never doubt His existence again, no matter what happens to you in the future.

Now, if you persevere, committing to loving and serving God whether you further experience His presence again or not, your spiritual journey will continue. It will continue with periods of sublime mystical experience, followed by periods of profound mystical darkness. That is how your prayer life will continue. How long and how often these times come and go depend not on you but on God, as you become more and more passive and He becomes more and more active in the work of purifying and refining you for union with Himself. And remember, you can cut and run at any time, as the majority do. But let me be clear, your perseverance is crucial.

Chapter 15

The Perfect Therapist

Let me explain why the experience of God's presence is suddenly followed by darkness, and darkness is suddenly followed by light. Contemplative prayer began because God's love has drawn your free will away from its ability to control the mind, the memory, and the imagination in meditation. Now, after experiencing the presence of God's love in the Prayer of Quiet and Full Union for some time, a similar thing takes place. God so draws your free will towards Himself and with such power that your free will is once more enthralled and captivated by God's love, but far more powerfully than before. So powerfully that, it not only loses its power over the mind, the memory, and the imagination in prayer, as it did before, but much more. For now your free will, that from time immemorial has been used to keep the door to the entrance of your unconscious closed, loses its power and that door opens. Now, the source and cause of the sins that we fall into in the conscious mind rise up to be seen as never before. This experience leads back into darkness where your sinfulness has to be seen, and, as it is seen, it can overwhelm the receiver and generate more powerful temptations than ever before, some of which lead the 'mystic' into sin.

As these sins are seen and confessed, the mystic must once more journey on in the darkness using The Prayer of the Heart. Then, thankfully the free will is free to close the door to the unconscious again. However, in God's time not yours, His powerful presence returns once more for a repeat of what happened before. So, the spiritual life of a mystic who practises contemplation alternates between hot and cold, light and darkness, presence and absence, and all to one end, and that is so that a sinful human being can be gradually purified and refined by the Holy Spirit, so that he or she can be united with Christ, as they originally desired. Christ called Himself a physician who came to heal sinners. He then sent the Holy Spirit, the perfect psychiatrist, to first show them the source of all sin in the nether regions of their personalities, while supporting them with His love. Then, He gradually helps them to face up to and overcome their sinfulness with His love. There is no need to spend a fortune on therapists in the mystic way. The Holy Spirit provides His services free! Furthermore, He not only helps a person back to what is considered to be normality, but to sanctity. How? Because in addition to destroying sin at source, His love contains within it all the infused virtues that no other therapist can give.

It is easy to give the impression that the fruits of contemplation are only given when a person begins to experience what I have called 'the contemplation of light': that is, when it is possible to experience the presence of God sometimes to shattering degrees of intensity. But that is not true. From the very beginning of what I have called 'the mystic way,' when the Holy Spirit first draws us towards God, contemplation begins and continues for those who persevere. This is a fact even if you do not seem to experience anything more than dryness and aridity while being plagued by a hundred and one distractions. The only reason to believe that God is in this strange new form of prayer is that there is, despite all else, a genuine desire for God even though that desire does not seem to be reciprocated.

Now the believer must first learn to travel onward, not by feelings but by faith. That is why at this stage of their journey contemplation is often referred to as 'The Prayer of Naked Faith'. No matter what you may feel as you try to journey onward, if your desire for God is continually sustained, even if by little more than your physical presence and 'The Prayer of the Heart', then your heart is open to receive the fruits of contemplation. They come to you through the love of God because they are contained within the love of God, and can percolate through what you only see as darkness because your heart's desire is clearly open to receive them. Naturally, the more you are purified and refined the more fully you are open to receive them in ever greater measure. But as long as you persevere, you begin to receive them in some measure from the beginning. I have already pointed out that after some time, although you may still be unable to make sense of this new form of prayer, you begin to realise that you would be worse off without it because you do seem to receive some spiritual strength to support you in your moral life.

Furthermore, although you still do not seem to have made sense of this new form of prayer, you do begin to receive a certain spiritual wisdom that you did not have before, although this is usually only seen with hindsight. The more you persevere then, the more your purification enables you to receive the Love of God, together with the infused virtues and the gifts and fruits of the Holy Spirit contained within it, even before God's love becomes tangible. The truth of the matter is, you have begun to practise divine loving, the loving that goes on giving whether it receives something in return or not. God cannot but resist returning this perfect form of love, and with ever greater fullness, as your journey unfolds. This is the only form of love in which a human being can learn through practice that it will eventually unite them with God after first uniting them with Christ.

After travelling in this way for very many years, continually practising the same sort of selfless sacrificial loving that Christ practised, whether in darkness or in light, you will eventually be sufficiently purified. You will be sufficiently purified for what western mystical writers tend to call the Mystical or the Spiritual Marriage, or what eastern mystical writers tend to call *Theosis* or Divinization. Prior to the Mystical Marriage, St Teresa of Avila explains that what she calls 'The Spiritual Betrothals' take place. Here for the first time the sensible feelings and the emotions that have been sufficiently purified, in what St John of the Cross calls 'The Dark Night of the Soul', can once more operate, as they did in meditation before the commencement of Contemplation. This is a preamble to the Mystical Marriage when we are spiritually and physically united with Christ, when our whole selves - body, blood, soul and humanity - are united with Christ, with His whole self, body, blood, soul and divinity. Then, we begin to contemplate God more perfectly than ever before because we are more perfectly united with Him and with His loving contemplation of the Father than ever before. Now at the highest peak possible of our spiritual journey on earth, we are open to receive more fully and more completely than ever before the fruits of contemplation. In so far as perfection is possible here on earth, then you could say you have arrived at perfection. But don't throw your passport away, for the journey is not yet over!

It is important to realise that the mystic way is not some sort of extraordinary way for spiritual oddities. It is the place where we learn to practise the selfless, sacrificial loving that was the very essence of

Christ's life on earth that was brought to its completion on the Cross. The mystic way is the way we imitate Him in such a way that we can be united with Him in His sacrificial act of loving. If this loving is not learnt in this life, then it must be learnt in the next life in purgatory. For until we have freely chosen to fully learn divine loving, we cannot be united with God in whom this divine loving is seen to perfection.

In one of her appearances in the last century, Our Lady said that God does not send anyone to purgatory because it is our choice. If we do not choose to learn divine loving in this life, that can alone unite us with God then it must be learnt in the next life in purgatory before union with God can take place in what we have traditionally come to call heaven. In the same way, Our Lady said that God does not send anyone to Hell. It is our choice if we choose permanently to turn away from learning the only form of loving that can unite us with God.

I would like to make one final point before leaving this chapter. When at the beginning of the 'mystic way' you may experience darkness and endless distractions, and at moments when, in darkness later on, the purification is seriously testing, prudence is necessary. Prudence is necessary to ensure that you do not pray for too long, for you could suffer from spiritual burnout and give up the journey. Later, in what I have called the contemplation of light, you could pray all day and with ease and be spiritually invigorated. This is the point when the benefit of a good and experienced spiritual director is needed. But sadly, today they are a very rare commodity. I never found one, and so I turned to Our Lady to be my mentor and to the Holy Spirit to guide my every step.

Part 4 Sacrifice

Chapter 16

Christ Teaches Contemplation by Example

When Christ turned to His Father each day in profound contemplative prayer, it was not just to love and worship Him, as He had done from Eternity in His divine nature, but to seek His help to support and sustain Him. It enabled Him to face and destroy the powers of evil that threatened His human nature. But the powers of evil that threatened to destroy Him did not rise from His fallen nature, as they do with us, because there was no sin in Him. They rose up against Him from the fallen human natures of those He came to redeem with His love. It was the very antithesis of love rising up in His own people that both threatened and finally put Him to death, a death that despite them was swallowed up in victory.

Jesus received help and strength from the Holy Spirit every evening in profound mystical contemplation. "He would *always* go off to some place where He could be alone and pray" (Luke 5:16). While He was at prayer, His apostles went fishing, rested or amused themselves to slow down after the day's work. However, their time would come. Just before the Ascension, Jesus told them that they were to go out into the world baptising, preaching, and teaching, so that He could continue His work of redemption through them. In order that they could be strengthened, supported and inspired, as He had been, He sent the Holy Spirit on the first Pentecost day. Now they were drawn up into Him into His mystical Body to contemplate the Father, as He did before them. Unlike Jesus, they were sinners and it would take many years repenting, praying, and making sacrifices before they were ready to go out to transform the world in His name.

Unfortunately, we do not have any record of their inner spiritual preparation and purification, as would be detailed by later mystics, but we know for certain that they did have to undergo a profound purification. We know this thanks to St Paul, because he wrote these words that are most revealing:

"I know a man in Christ who, fourteen years ago, was caught up - whether still in or out of the body, I do not know; God knows - right into the third heaven. I do know, however, that this same person - whether in or out of the body; God knows, was caught up into paradise and heard things that cannot, must not be put into human language" (2 Corinthians 12 :1-5).

Now, St Paul could not have had such profound mystical experiences without a long and exacting purification. If you want to know the precise nature of his mystical experiences, then you would need to read *The Interior Castle* by St Teresa of Avila. Then, you would need to read *The Dark Night of the Soul* by St John of the Cross to understand the purification that he had to undergo before he would be sufficiently ready to receive such sublime supernatural gifts. These mystical graces would have prepared him to receive the fruits of contemplation that shine through everything that he wrote, everything that he said and did. That is not to mention the appalling physical sufferings He had to endure throughout his life, and a martyr's death at the end of it. Although we do not find similar details of mystical experiences from the writings of the other apostles, we do know that they experienced them too, as we can see the fruits of contemplation in all they wrote and did. Add to this the sufferings that they had to endure throughout their lives, and the terrible deaths they were forced to experience at the end of it, as can be read in the Acts of the Apostles and the Acts of the Martyrs.

The same is true of the Fathers of the Church whose writings are still the bedrock of our Catholic faith. That the Church is at present full of would-be apostles eager to do what the first apostles did for the Church is clearly evident. Sadly, what is not so evident is that they are prepared to do what their predecessors did. Both born Catholics or recent converts seem to think that a religious conversion, albeit genuine, is a call to set out without delay to become the spiritual leaders for which they have not been prepared. The first apostles had profound and personal experience of God's love through Christ Himself, but they still believed they had to spend many years of penance and repentance learnt in 'the desert' before they had the effrontery to set themselves up to lead and guide others.

Chapter 17

Christ's Daily Liturgy of Sacrificial Loving

When Greek converts saw what Christ did to save humanity, they used a Greek word to describe His redemptive action. Let me explain. When an Athenian citizen, for instance, performed a great act of public service for the whole community, it was called his liturgy. So, when Greek converts saw the great public service that Christ had performed throughout His life on earth for the whole of Humanity, they called it His Liturgy. However, they did not just want to stand back and admire how He lived and died whilst He was on earth; they wanted to follow His example and take up their cross and imitate Him. In order to do this, they were taught how to meditate, so that they could come to know and love Him more deeply. Then, in coming to know Him more deeply, they would come to love Him in such a way that His Love, sent on the first Pentecost Day, would take them up and into Him, into His mystical body inspiring them from within to live, love, and die as He had. Like the other Christians who were led into the mystic way, they would have to fight against the power of evil, as He did.

But for them, that evil did not just come from others and from the world they lived in, but from within themselves. But the love of the Holy Spirit who they received through contemplation, continually sustained them, as they experienced absence and presence, light and darkness, and sorrow and joy just as Jesus did. In fact, this is how they daily took up their cross to follow Him. This was the inner nature of what they called the 'white martyrdom', or the daily dying to self which they joyfully accepted in order to continually take up their cross in order to follow Him. This is how, first and foremost, they came to practise the profound sacrificial and contemplative spirituality that Christ Himself had first practised before introducing it to the first Christian community. It was a sacrificial spirituality that differed from that of the contemporary Jews because the offering made to God was not livestock or the produce of the land, but themselves.

Furthermore, it was offered in the New Temple, which is Christ Himself. And, because this offering was spiritual rather than physical, Christ called it a 'New Worship in Spirit and in Truth' when He was talking to the Samaritan woman. This new offering was nothing other than the offering of themselves, made continually everyday of their lives. That is why they came to see that in the New Temple, in which Christ is the High Priest, they themselves were priests, because only they could make the offering of themselves through all and everything they did each day. That is why their daily *Shema*, their Morning Offering, was so important to them, because just as Christ Himself used it to consecrate everything He said and did to God each day, they did likewise in imitation of Him. However, they did not just offer everything they said and did to God, in, with, and through Christ, every day of their lives, they did something further. Let me explain what I mean.

On the night before He died, Christ did something utterly sublime that took place at the Last Supper. Anticipating what would happen to Him the next day, when His life on earth was completed by His death and glorification, He took ordinary bread and wine and consecrated it. He consecrated it in such a way that the whole of His Life, Death, and Glorification became present under the appearance of bread and wine. Those who first received their Saviour into them on that Holy Night were told to do what Christ Himself did in memory of Him in the future. Those who have studied Hebrew or Aramaic will know that 'to remember' something from the past for the Jews does not just mean to call it to mind, but to make it happen again now in the present. And that is precisely what the first Christians did later, on Sunday, the first day of the week. Once a week they would gather to celebrate what came to be called the Eucharist and what we more usually call the Mass. Then, as promised, Christ came amongst His people again in the Sacred Mysteries. He was there as surely as He was there in the Upper Room on the Night before He died. He was there under the appearance of Bread and Wine, the same Christ, who sacrificed His whole life and His death for all.

The Christians who gathered for these Sacred Mysteries had spent their previous week trying to imitate the way that Christ had lived on earth, sacrificing themselves for Him in all that they said and did. They understood this to be the way they would carry their daily crosses in imitation of Him, practising the New Worship in Spirit and in Truth that He practised throughout his life on earth. This they saw as His Liturgy, His great act of public service for the whole of Humanity. Now, this continuing act of Sacrifice, Christ's Liturgy that he practised through blood sweat and tears every day of his life, was made present each week at the weekly Eucharist or Mass, so that they could unite their daily liturgy, practised in imitation of Christ, with His sacred and sacrificial liturgy.

The Supernatural life and love that they received in return from God, as they offered themselves and the daily crosses that they had carried, gave them the grace to continue imitating Christ in the forthcoming week. This ever-recurring weekly dynamic constituted the profound mystical, sacrificial, and contemplative spirituality that made a greater percentage of the population into saints than at any other time in history. In the year one hundred and twenty, St Justin who finally died as a martyr, summed up how this spirituality was both understood and practised in life and in death by the first Christians. When at the end of the great Eucharistic prayer the celebrant said, "In Him, with Him, through Him, in the unity of the Holy Spirit, all honour and glory to you almighty Father", the 'Amen' recited by the congregation nearly took the roof off. Two hundred years later, St Jerome said virtually the same thing, this time using slightly different words. When the great Amen was proclaimed by the congregation it sounded, he said, "like a thunderclap" that resounded around the Basilica." Also, the people who were totally aware of their priesthood were not just giving their assent to a prayer with which they agreed, but proclaiming loud and clear their adherence to a profound inner and mystical way of life. It was a way of life in which they daily took up their crosses in order to follow and imitate Christ and His Liturgy of love that He first practised in all that He said and did.

Chapter 18

The Consequence of Love Lost

When, as we have seen, the meditation that led to contemplation was seriously undermined by Arianism and Iconoclasm, there came terminal change in the Christian Spirituality previously practised in the Catholic Church. If Christ was not divine, then meditating on His humanity was not enough. For, in meditating on His humanity alone, no matter how great He might be, He was just another dead man. It was only in meditating on His divine and His human nature together as one, that the love generated there enabled the Holy Spirit, who bound the two together, to lead a person onwards and into contemplation. In meditating on the Christ who once lived in the past, they were raised up to contemplate Him in the present. Here, at one with Him in His risen glory, they could contemplate "Almighty God our common Father."

Without meditation, the door to Contemplation and the profound spirituality practised by the first Christians simply disappeared. The Mass of course continued, but it was no longer the place where 'ordinary' Catholics offered themselves through Christ to the Father in the same radical way that they did in the first three or more centuries. The daily sacrifices that used to be made in learning 'divine loving' in contemplative prayer were no longer practised as before, and so were no longer the vital acts of sacrificial loving that could be united with Christ's great sacrifice at Mass. Through the Dark Ages, the profound mystical dynamic that prevailed in the early Church might have been lost to sight for the majority of Catholic laity, but it nevertheless continued in the Monasteries. That is, until after the victory of the first Crusade in 1099 when vast numbers of pilgrims returned to Europe filled with a new spirituality centred on the person of Jesus Christ. Devotion to the Humanity of Christ was rekindled and once again meditation on Christ's life led to Contemplation and ushered in six centuries in which contemplative spirituality returned to Catholicism. It was as we have seen, in the aftermath of the condemnation of the pseudo mysticism called Quietism, that the meditation that led to Contemplation was once more undermined.

Molinos, the founder of Quietism, had been leading his flock into a pseudo-mysticism that took them back to Protestantism and into gross sexual depravity for which he was condemned to life imprisonment in 1687, as you can read in Monsignor Ronald Knox's book *Enthusiasm.* The consequent moral decline in the Church grew with every subsequent century. It was to call us back to deep prayer and the return to moral probity, long lost, that Our Lady appeared at Fatima and elsewhere, for the Church had been gradually dying ever since the love of God had been taken out of Catholic Spirituality in the immediate aftermath of Quietism.

The Mystical Theology that was taught and explained by the greatest number of front rank mystical writers that the Church has ever known, suddenly disappeared almost overnight. The disaster that followed has gathered pace and with ever greater momentum down to the present day.

Before Quietism, Systematic theology and Mystical theology were complementary. Systematic theology taught the mind how to know God while Mystical theology taught the heart how to love Him. After the condemnation of Quietism, Mystical theology disappeared from Catholic education from the top down. Two and a half centuries later, I asked the theologian who taught me to give a course on Mystical theology. His answer shattered me. He said, "I know nothing at all about mystical theology". After inquiring assiduously in subsequent years, I discovered that he had been speaking for almost all other theologians. When you take love out of any family, including the Church, then it simply disintegrates. The outer shell might remain intact, but the inner life has gone.

Sadly that is what we seem to see all too often in the Church today. Before the Second Vatican Council, many of my fellow students had followed St John Henry Newman back to the early Church to look for a solution. They thought they had found it in the early Liturgy that was reintroduced at the Second Vatican Council. But sadly they, and the scholars who reintroduced it were equally ignorant of the mystical theology that was taken out of Catholic Spirituality after Quietism. Their ignorance meant that they were unable to see that it was the profound sacrificial and contemplative spirituality that found its expression in the early Liturgy, that was not just its foundation but its heart and soul. It was the leaven that made it rise, the salt that gave it savour.

This ignorance was shared by all the Bishops and expert theologians who came to the Second Vatican Council. I have been unable to find one exception. It ensured that the Document on the Liturgy had no prequel explaining the sublime mystical spirituality of the early Church. The practical consequences of this has meant that, down to the present day, both sheep and shepherds have been denied the supernatural God-given spirituality that Our Lord first practised Himself before introducing it to the early Christians who joyfully followed Him by carrying their daily crosses. In short, there has remained a deadly dislocation between the expression of God's divine love in the Mass and the way in which that divine loving is daily practised and learnt in prayer. This not only affected my fellow students, but all subsequent attempts to renew the Church by other well-meaning but ignorant Catholic leaders.

Today, more and more Catholics tend to define their identity by their liturgical preferences without any reference to the inner spiritual life that is expressed in the liturgy. In fact, Liturgy seems to be the main talking point as the instrument of renewal in the modern Church. How sad then that the vast majority seem to have decisive and set ideas about the Liturgy but with little, if any, knowledge to substantiate what depends far more on feelings than facts. For instance, a four-man camera team who have produced a major documentary on the Mass and travelled over 6,000 miles to interview me, had never read the classical, two-part masterwork on the Mass by Father Joseph Jungmann SJ. His two volume work *The Mass of the Roman Rite* is generally considered to be the greatest work on the history of the Mass. Although the first part of their film tended to emphasise the subjective, the sentimental, and the superficial at the expense of the factual, the historical, and the theological, the second part was more helpful. It showed clearly how the influence of humanism in the guise of freemasonry tried to change the traditional Mass in what came to be called the Novus Ordo Missae. It tried to take out the emphasis on the sacrificial nature of the Mass, making it instead into a memorial meal to remember a great human being whose moral teaching should be cherished.

However, let me turn to the profound inner life of the faithful, without which the Liturgy has no vital spiritual foundation.

Chapter 19

The Meaning of Our Redemption

It was because His disciples could not bear the very thought that He would have to suffer death, that Jesus did not explain the meaning of why and how He would have to suffer before His time finally came. But one of the very first things that He did after His Resurrection was explain why He had to suffer before entering into His glory to two of His disciples on the road to Emmaus. They immediately told the Apostles back in Jerusalem what was in effect the true meaning of His redemptive action.

In order to understand the profound meaning of redemptive suffering let me turn to Chapter Seven of the Letter of St Paul to the Romans, where St Paul describes the dilemma that slavery to sin has put him in. He writes, "I have been sold as a slave to sin. I cannot understand my own behaviour. I cannot do the things that I want to do, and I find myself doing the very things that I hate. For though the will to do what is good is within me, the performance of it is not, with the result that instead of doing the good things that I want to do, I find myself doing the sinful things that I do not want" (Romans 7:14-20). This is why St Paul said that he has been sold into the slavery of sin. Anybody who is imprisoned in physical slavery can be redeemed by money, but money cannot redeem a person who is imprisoned into spiritual slavery. Something far more valuable, something far more powerful than money is required, and that something else is called love. Not our own love, for that is not powerful enough, but God's love, that Jesus Christ Our Lord received in all its fullness on the first Easter day and communicated to us on the first Pentecost Day. However, so that there may be no misunderstanding about the meaning of our redemption, let me make something quite clear. The love that Christ received from the Father to redeem us, could not possibly have been given to the devil as payment for our redemption, because the devil cannot possibly receive it. This love was given to us, or more precisely, it is given to us as we try to receive it. So, this love of God, the Holy Spirit, which was continually empowering Christ whilst He was on earth to combat the devil, can do the same for us. What Jesus explained to His disciples on the road to Emmaus was how He obtained that fullness of love that redeemed us from slavery to sin. Let me explain how this was done. As the scriptures tell us that Jesus was like us in all things but sin, He was therefore tempted as we are, not only at the beginning of His public ministry in the desert, but also in the Garden of Gethsemane and on the cross at the end of it. However, what we do not see is that He was also tempted throughout His life by those who hated Him and wanted to destroy Him. Unlike us, every time He was tempted, He turned away from the sin that could have enslaved Him to evil. At the same time, He turned to God who filled Him with His Love.

His whole life then became a supernatural stream of seamless acts of loving as He endlessly turned away from evil and turned to receive the love of God instead. The moment that His life on earth came to an end was therefore also the moment when He was filled to over-flowing with the love of God. The reservoir of love that filled Him after a life of endless loving was further filled to overflowing by the ocean of God's love that He then poured out and onto others on the first Pentecost day.

This enabled our weak human love to be suffused and surcharged with Divine Loving, giving us the strength to resist the evil that was irresistible without it. As this love can empower those who receive it to keep turning away from the slavery of sin and turn instead to God, it came to be called Redeeming Love. And, as this love of God comes to us through Christ's lifelong loving, He came to be called The Redeemer. That is why He was called Jesus from the beginning, because Jesus means Saviour, or the One who saves us by redeeming us from the slavery of sin with His love.

True imitation of Christ Our Redeemer therefore means following the example of His redeeming loving while He was on earth. This means using the love that He continually gives to all who are open to receive it to keep turning away from the temptation to do evil and to keep turning towards God, or in the words of St Peter, to keep repenting. The sacrifices that we make in trying to do this are offered daily to God as Christ did. Then, on Sundays the first Christians would join together to offer all the sacrifices that they made during the previous week, in, with, and through Christ their Redeemer, whose complete Sacrifice is made present in Him in the sacred mysteries of the Mass.

Christ's explanation of His Redemptive Suffering on earth that He explained on the road to Emmaus was of paramount importance. They understood why He had to suffer, but why they, His disciples and future disciples would have to likewise suffer if they wanted to share in His redemptive action for others, and that of course means us. Christ had to suffer because He had to face up to the diabolical evil in men that was bent on destroying Him before He could redeem mankind, as He did finally in winning the last decisive battle on the Cross. The evil in those same men, and in others who would follow them, would try to destroy His disciples too. But there would be another source of evil that Christ Himself did not have to confront but that His disciples would, namely, the evil in themselves born of original sin and their own personal sinfulness. That is why His Apostles and His disciples had to spend several years 'in retreat,' praying, and in their prayer facing up to the evil in themselves. The redemptive suffering that they had to endure facing up to, and fighting against the evil in others and the evil within themselves, was offered up at their weekly Mass. It was here that they offered up their sufferings together with the lifelong redemptive sufferings of their Risen Lord, who once more not only came amongst them, but entered into them surcharging them with His love for the ongoing battle ahead, as He Himself had been continually suffused with His Father's love while He was on earth. That is why, as Christ explained at the Last Supper, He was a man of joy as they would become men of joy too despite the sufferings involved in daily taking up their cross to follow Him.

Sadly, in recent years, leaders of what has been called the 'new remnant' seem to be far more interested in the way Christ's lifelong act of redemptive sacrificial loving is celebrated in the Mass than in imitating it for themselves in their daily lives. The communal Liturgy used to express and embody Christ's redemptive action at Mass is the expression of the inner life of the Church, where the faithful live and die daily for Christ. If you take that inner life away, undermine it, or wrongly assume that it is there, it soon becomes little more than the outward expression for something that is not there, like the smile on the face of the Cheshire Cat in Alice in Wonderland. No matter how people try to make it meaningful in itself, and for themselves, it will soon become little more than gongs booming and symbols clashing, because without love learnt in prayer it will do little good.

Those who promote Liturgical Renewal and those who promote Charismatic Renewal have far more in common than they might think. They both seem to be far less interested in promoting the redemptive action of Christ in daily living and dying, inside and outside of prayer, than in celebrating it in liturgy. But whereas Charismatics tend to be spontaneous, adolescent, and artless, the Liturgists tend to be more measured, mature, and sophisticated. But they both seem to be far more interested in how to express their faith in their own chosen forms of liturgy than in how to live it, in daily carrying their cross in imitation of Christ's redeeming action while He was on earth.

The beautiful music, the Gregorian Chant, the sublime and ancient anthems, canticles, and hymns were mainly written as the outward expression of a living and vital Catholic spirituality that preceded the condemnation of Quietism. They were the expression of a profound and deep prayer life that now no longer exists. The fallacy of neo-liturgists is that they believe it is enough to reproduce the outward expression of that profound spirituality, without the spirituality itself as its foundation. It will never be enough. Without the continual offerings of love to God on every weekday, the offering of ourselves to God on Sunday will be no more than liturgy without love.

Until, beginning with themselves, they work to practise and reintroduce the profound redemptive and sacrificial spirituality that Christ first introduced into the early Church, they will continue to promote a liturgy that expresses little more than their own aesthetical sensibilities. It will lay them open to the criticism that Christ levelled against the liturgists of His day: "These people worship me with their lips but their hearts are far from me". In order to prevent his brothers falling into this same error, St Bernardine of Siena wrote these words in letters of gold around the sanctuary where they celebrated their liturgy, "*Si Cor non orat in vanum lingua laborat*": or "If the heart does not pray then the tongue labours in vain".

Chapter 20

Our Whole Lives Become the Mass

I recently spoke to a young man who had spent years trying to show how 'The Mass of Ages' should be celebrated in such a way that it should inspire all who participated in it, so that they would leave their weekly liturgy filled and overflowing with spiritual euphoria. But the Mass is not a concert. It is the vital living embodiment of the daily redemptive actions of Jesus Christ, from the wooden Crib in which He was born to the wooden Cross on which He died for us. It releases for all who are open to receive it, infinite loving, the infinite loving that flowed into Him the moment He gave His all for us on the cross. It is that loving that will enable us to continue to take up our cross in the fight against evil. If our weekly Mass does no more than make us feel good at the time, rather than inspiring us to continue the imitation of Christ at every moment of every day of the week ahead by practising what the first Christians called 'White Martyrdom', then something is wrong. No matter how correctly or wonderfully, the Sunday Liturgy is celebrated at Mass, if it does not inspire those who attend it to practise the self-same daily liturgy that

Christ Himself lived every day of His life on earth, then it has not achieved its objective. For, in the words of the great liturgist, Joseph Jungmann, "The whole purpose of the Mass is that the whole of our lives should become the Mass, the place where we continually offer ourselves up through Christ to God Our Father".

Long before we enter into the church for Sunday Mass, we should have spent the previous week making daily sacrifices to enable us to die to self in the battle against evil. This is what Our Lady asked us to do in her appearances in the last century. Without the daily sacrifices made in and out of prayer, we will not be able to unite ourselves with the sacrificial and redemptive offering of Christ made to His Father each time we go to Mass.

There is no evidence in the scriptures that Christ ever offered sacrifices in the Temple as His mother and foster father and as His own disciples did. That is because Our Lord came to introduce a new interior and more spiritual form of offering, the offering of oneself. The sacrifices that God really wanted in the future was not of sheep, or goats, or cattle, but the offering of ourselves to God, made every moment of every day of our lives, in and through all that we say and do. That is why the early Christians were so aware of their own priesthood, because only they could offer themselves to God. And the same, of course, applies to us.

Our Lord did not come to reconstitute the Old Worship then, but to introduce a new worship in Spirit and in Truth. This was the worship that He practised everyday of His life by doing His Father's will daily, and then by offering Himself to Him together with all that He said and did, despite the evil that tried to destroy Him. This new spiritual worship that He was the first to practise was supported and sustained by the profound contemplation to which He turned daily as we have seen (Luke 5:16). When we return to doing this, and doing it daily as the first Christians did, then we are back to the true imitation of Christ. Then at the weekly liturgy, we are able to unite our daily redemptive sacrifices made in trying to imitate Christ to Our Lord's Great Redemptive Sacrifice.

When St Paul said that he preached Christ and Christ crucified, he was reminding his listeners that they had all committed themselves to this new daily worship in Spirit and in Truth. It involved taking up their cross to follow Him, as they died to self each day when in the prayer beyond first beginnings, they endlessly practised saying 'no' to self and 'yes' to God, just as we do. This daily dying learnt in prayer enabled them to be transformed and transfigured by the love of their Risen Lord. It was this daily mystical dying to self that came to be called 'White Martyrdom'. G. K. Chesterton said, "It was not that Christianity has been tried and found wanting, but rather that it was found difficult and so left untried". This is precisely what he meant by the daily carrying of our cross with Christ in all that we say and do. This is particularly true when, after meditation, a person is led into Contemplation to begin learning how to love, as Christ did before us.

Unconditional sacrificial loving can only be learned by practising true selfless unconditional, sacrificial loving. Herein lies the essence of the cross that we are called upon to carry daily in imitation of Christ. That is why St Paul insisted that he preached Christ and Christ crucified (1 Corinthians 1:23). If this was a stumbling block to the Greeks and to the Jews, then it is sadly still a stumbling block to us. But it is the only way to renew the Church, not by endlessly trying to change the rites and rituals of the liturgy, the language in which it is celebrated, or the aesthetic way in which it is presented to the faithful. The aesthetic way in which the Liturgy is presented to the faithful is meaningless without the ascetical daily life lived by those who take part in it, in imitation of our Saviour Jesus Christ. A retreat master once told me that the most moving and meaningful Mass that he ever attended was in a prison camp. There, the chaplain had nothing other than a wooden bench for an altar, a small piece of bread, and a thimble full of wine with which to celebrate the sacred mysteries. Before the Mass was celebrated, their Chaplain had taught his fellow 'prisoners' how to use their daily sufferings in such a way that they could be united with the redemptive sufferings of Christ, before, during, and after Mass.

He taught them how to take their solitary sufferings, the heartaches, the hunger, and the humiliations, and with their comrades, unite them with the redemptive sufferings of Christ at Mass for their own redemption and for that of others. Then, how to receive from Christ's sacramental presence the support, succour, and strength to live out one more week, one more month, one more year, in imitation of their Saviour. The Psychiatrist Viktor Frankl, himself a prisoner of war in one of the most pernicious of all prison camps, said that a person could bear almost any suffering if it had meaning. Those Holy Masses in that prison camp gave so much meaning to what would otherwise have been four wasted years of pointless and painful suffering. My retreat master insisted that they had inspired him to become a priest to try to do for others what those Masses did for him.

In summary, this matter must be made quite clear or we will begin again being misled by pseudo liturgists, both amateur and professional. For they primarily proclaim above all else the importance of how Christ's daily selfless living, giving, dying, and death on the cross should be perfectly celebrated in rite and rituals, sign and symbols. They do not primarily teach how, first and foremost, we must imitate His selfless living, giving, dying, and death on the cross in our daily lives through, in the words of Our Lady, daily repentance, prayer and sacrifice. If they had personal experiential knowledge of the prayer, through meditation to contemplation, where divine, selfless, redemptive loving is learnt, then the Holy Spirit would impel them not to concentrate on the outside of the cup, but on what Christ called the inside of the cup. That is the daily redemptive suffering and dying that He told His disciples that they would have to accept in imitation of Him. Those who imitate Him in doing this do not have to be told how to participate in the Mass with humility, reverence, and awe. We must beware of being led into the future by neo scribes and Pharisees who, like their predecessors, put Christ to death. They put Christ to death because He saw through their superficial externalism that concentrated on the outside, not on the inside, of the cup from which Christ and His first followers chose to drink in order to do the will of God their Father.

Some time ago, a modern mystic was complaining to Christ in prayer that, for all his life he had to contend with the vast majority of Catholics for whom their faith had become little more than external observance. Christ's reply came immediately, "That too was the story of my life, and of my death, for trying to preach the truth". Without the continual offerings of ourselves to God on every weekday, the offering of ourselves to God on Sunday will be no more than liturgy without love.

Chapter 21

A Mother's Loving Message

The aftermath of Quietism not only changed the nature of the liturgy, but of personal piety too. Once the faithful were no longer inspired to meditate as their first Christian forebears were, then the door to the Mystic way and to contemplation was closed to them. The gap was filled by a plethora of devotions, spiritual exercises, and an unhealthy fascination with private revelations, none of which were necessarily bad in themselves, but they were excentric. They are excentric in the literal meaning of the word because they lead the faithful away from the central Catholic perennial spirituality given to us by Jesus Christ Our Lord that I have summarised in this book. In modern times, they have become so commonplace and so diverse that they have led to the expression 'A Cafeteria Spirituality'.

Just before leaving the Last Supper for Gethsemane, Christ's prayer for us was that we may be one in Him, as He was in the Father and the Father was in Him. Sadly, since Quietism, Catholics have progressively made Christ's prayer ineffective. Even His prayer cannot force His will on those who prefer to follow their own. Their own wills have led them to choose their own spiritualities as children choose their own goodies at the pick and mix counter in the supermarket. And in doing this, far from fulfilling the prayer of Christ, they are all different. You will hardly find two Catholics alike today in the spirituality that once made their first forebears one. All have their own favourite devotions, their own self chosen spiritual exercises, their own devotion to this or that saint or religious order, to their private revelations, or to their own best loved liturgical practices. They are all mixed together in a unique spiritual cocktail that, like all cocktails, may enable them to feel good, but prevent them from living the only true perennial spirituality to which we must return without delay, because it was first lived and practised by Christ Himself before He gave it to the Church 'in perpetuity'.

Although we seem to be in an unholy mess, the answer to our present plight is immediately open to all who seriously want to return to the selfless sacrificial, redemptive and contemplative Spirituality that was not just lived by the first saints, but by all the saints who followed them. The saints who should be our inspiration and our guide did not base their spirituality on that of previous saints, on the private and questionable revelations of dubious previous mystics, or on their own personal liturgical preferences, but on coming to know and love Jesus Christ and living the spirituality that He bequeathed to the early Church. There is however, yet another group of onetime Catholics, who, seeing that neither a new liturgy, nor new private revelations, nor a mixture of old devotional practices, nor trying to mix and match self-chosen strands of spirituality lifted piecemeal from different religious orders will achieve anything, have gone in a different direction. Blind to the true tradition, thanks again to Quietism, they condemn all tradition and seek salvation instead from the latest, 'up-to-datest' wisdom of the world.

Do not wait for some sort of initiative from the top in the Church, which I promise will never come, or even for some sort of divine intervention. Make it your personal choice now. Such a choice was made many years ago by a semi-literate son of a draper. He so turned to and based his life on that of Christ, he came to be called 'The Second Christ.' His name was St Francis of Assisi. The same happened to a young woman. Like St Francis, she gave three years to turning back to Christ, and she did it without leaving her own home. Her name was St Catherine of Siena. Both these semi-literate saints changed the world of their day and in such a short time; St Francis was forty-five when he died and St Catherine thirty-three. They are now both joint patron saints of Italy. If you decided to give your life radically over to God, following the Spirituality that he gave to His Son, there is no question that you could follow in their footsteps, not because you are a saint, but because, like them to begin with, you are a sinner. But also like them, you radically open yourself to the Holy Spirit. If you alone do this, then the spiritual repercussions could be enormous, but if several of you decided to do this together in the same parish, then the repercussions, could be epoch-making, not just for yourselves or your parish, but for your country and for the world, who in you, will see once more what the power of God can do working through weakness.

Let me end by summing up all that I have said by recourse to the greatest modern theologian speaking today. That theologian is Our Lady the Mother of God and Our Mother too. If you have not been able to follow all that I have said, just listen to her and to the simple message that she has been repeating to those who would listen in recent years. Remember, she taught Jesus how to pray as her parents had taught her to pray. She listened more attentively than any other to His profound teaching. She was there in person to see Him die on the Cross and there too on the first Pentecost day to both see and receive the outpouring of the Holy Spirit. Although those who first received the Holy Spirit on the birthday of the Church, and subsequently, including the Apostles, needed time and even years before they could be sufficiently prepared and purified to receive the Holy Spirit as Christ intended, Mary, His mother was different. As she was immaculately conceived and so there was no sin in her, she was instantly reunited with her Son in His new glorified and mystical body.

Whenever she turned to contemplative prayer, she was not just united with her son in love, but united with Him in his contemplative loving of His Father to receive in abundance the fruits of Contemplation. When the first Christians looked at her, they saw where they would be going if they listened to the call to continual repentance that she and the first apostles preached to all who wished to be filled with the Holy Spirit. That they did listen can be seen in the history of the early Church, for it was only with the fruits of Contemplation that those first Christians transformed a pagan Roman Empire into a Christian Empire in such a short time. What was done then can and will be done again, if we only listen to the simple message which is, to repent, pray, make sacrifices, and then offer those sacrifices together with the Redemptive Sacrifices made for us by her son.

Remember, repentance, unlike conversion, is not a once or twice in a lifetime affair, but as the Aramaic word for repentance makes clear, it is an ever continuing process of turning back to God every day and every moment of our lives, in all that we say and do. The prayer to which she calls us is, in the first instance, the place where the repentance to which we are called is practised at speed. As St Teresa of Avila makes abundantly clear, we will always have distractions and temptations in prayer, thus giving us the opportunity to practise loving God by the way we continually turn away from them. This is how we learn to love, as God loves us, and as Christ loves us, by making acts of love in what St Angela of Foligno calls the School of Divine Love. The first and most important sacrifices that we freely choose to make in our life are those we make in creating quality daily time in which to love God each day, by practising what I have called 'divine loving' inside the contemplative prayer to which we are all called. This of course means radically cutting down on the time we waste daily as slaves to the Mass Media in its myriad forms.

The rightly renowned psychiatrist, Vicktor Frankl, said that you can bear almost anything if it has a meaning, so let me explain why you have to experience so much darkness and aridity at the beginning of contemplative prayer. When the Holy Spirit first leads you into the beginning of Contemplation to begin the process of purification for union with God, without fully realising it, you have previously been predominantly acting selfishly. You have been acting selfishly in such a way that your character has developed a self-centred propensity that has become a habit that must be reversed if you are ever to be united with God. That is why, by using the prayer of the heart you keep making God-centred acts of love so that in time you gradually develop a God-centred propensity that eventually becomes a habit, enabling you to keep turning to God with ease and facility to receive his love in return. This is the love that contains within it the fruits of Contemplation that can not only change you, but also others who receive this love through you. However, this usually takes years rather than months, because selfishness is entrenched within us, and only persistent perseverance in making selfless acts of loving God in darkness and aridity, surrounded by distractions and temptation, can reverse the selfishness that has become a habit. That is why the majority turn away from the opportunity to carry their daily cross in imitation of Christ's redemptive action and return to the prayer of beginners, if they do not give up prayer, and even their faith, entirely. If you persevere, you are in fact participating in the redeeming action of Christ

Himself as He kept turning to love His Father despite the darkness and aridity, despite the distractions and temptations that He had to experience too, not just in the desert, in Gethsemane, and on the Cross, but throughout His life on earth. This is the true imitation of Christ that enables you to carry your daily cross behind Him in such a way that you are united with His redeeming action, for your own salvation and for that of others. Furthermore, it enables you to make reparation for the selfish and self-centred acts that turned you away from Christ in the past, and for the reparation of the sins of others. That is what you are doing at the beginning of Contemplation when you are tempted to believe that you are doing nothing and what little you are doing is pointless and purposeless.

When these sufferings and sacrifices are united to the great Redemptive Sacrifice that Christ made when we go to Mass, we receive to the measure of our giving, enabling us to pursue our spiritual journey even more deeply in the coming week. As this weekly mystical dynamic continues and deepens, week in week out, year in year out, then we are taken up ever more deeply into the mystery of Christ's redemptive action, and He in turn is able to continue the work of redemption through us for the world that can never be changed without Him. That is why the sublime spirituality of the early Church involved above all else the daily practice of learning divine loving in prayer where the faithful learnt the selfless unconditional loving practised throughout His life on earth by Jesus Christ Our Lord. This loving is both sacrificial and redemptive for those who practise it, and for others too for whom Christ continues to redeem through us. This whole mystical dynamic is perfectly summed up in what Our Lord called 'The New Worship in Spirit and in Truth'. This profound spiritual worship is practised within the New Temple, which is Christ Himself, and through Him because He is the New High Priest through whom we are fully open to the love of the Father. It is this love and this love alone that contains within it all the infused virtues and gifts of the Holy Spirit to make all things possible that are quite impossible without them. Now, perhaps we can see more clearly than ever what is meant by the profound contemplative, sacrificial, and redemptive spirituality, practised by the first Christians, to which we must return without delay, or we will continue in free fall to the inevitable disaster that awaits us.

Chapter 22

Perfection

Thanks to the Incarnation, Christ was able to draw others into Himself to experience, through His divinized human nature, something of what He had experienced before His Incarnation, namely the love of the Three in One. This is God's plan conceived from all eternity for us, so that we would find our ultimate destiny in eternal life and everlasting loving, in what, as we have seen, St Paul called God's secret plan, the *Mysterion.*

When His apostles saw Christ transfigured on Mount Tabor, they were being given a preview, not just of what would happen to Him after the Resurrection, but what would happen to His followers too, not just in the next life, but even in this life, if they persevered in the spiritual life leading them ever more deeply into His sacred humanity. For, be sure of this, the spiritual life that we pursue in prayer takes us up, after purification, into His sacred and transformed and transfigured humanity to experience His perfect human love for us. Further to this we also encounter there those loved ones who have also been taken up and into his glorified human nature. Nor do we travel on beyond His glorified body for this is the place where we reside to eternity, gazing in, with, and through Him on the glory of the Three in One where He was begotten from eternity and only left briefly to take us back with Him to the place where we were first conceived, where we will find our ultimate destiny.

In this life, the mystic who has reached what the Eastern Fathers called divinization, or *Theosis*, will at one moment be transported physically by the love of their risen Lord, and at another moment be transported with Him into the ecstatic joy of contemplating our Loving Father. The thrilling, enthralling, and transforming experience of human loving at its most perfect can be suddenly followed by the supra human loving with which Christ loves His Father that envelops a person and draws them into ecstatic bliss. It is here where only in an otherworldly silence, does God communicate what His Son came to give us. Words unite those who are separated from each other, but in the perfect union with God that has been our deepest desire from the beginning, there is a perfect infinite and blissful silence.

But all has not yet been said about our journey into the profound mystical vortex of loving that revolves between the Father and the Son. It is into this final mystery that we will all be caught up and to all eternity. I say 'we' because we are not alone. We are at one with all who have chosen to enter into this ecstatic joy, with mothers and fathers, brothers and sisters, friends and lovers, children and grandchildren, and not just our extended family, but the whole extended Christian family, living, and dead. They are not just living with us in Christ, but also travelling with us into never-ending beatitude. Our own personal joy and satisfaction is enhanced beyond our wildest dreams by re-meeting our own families again in Christ's own glorified and mystical body and in knowing and loving them as never before. Even in the best of families, the pernicious cancer of selfishness prevented us loving each other as we would have wished while we were on earth. But now that the cancer has been purified away and we have been transfused with pure love, there is nothing to prevent us from becoming the genuine loving families that we always wanted to be, but never really were on earth. Nevertheless, this supernatural and transforming reunion with our families in the next life is not the end of our journey, but the prelude to a new journey as we set out together upon our final and unending journey into eternal life and loving, where God's plan for us from the beginning, his *Mysterion*, is brought to perfection.

Together, we will not just experience the fullness of ecstatic joy, but the ever more fulfilling joy of experiencing *Epecstasy*. In order to express our ultimate destination, St Gregory of Nyssa, the great mystical poet devised a new word by adding a prefix to the word ecstasy to create: *Epecstasy*. This word means that we not only go out of ourselves into God through an ever-deepening love, but that we continually go out of ourselves and into God through love - through His infinite love and to eternity. For the more God's infinite loving enters into us, then the more the capacity to receive even more love grows within us and continues to grow to all eternity as we relentlessly go beyond and supersede what was once our capacity for love. As this journey unfolds, our capacity to receive and give love never stops expanding as we travel without any further let or hindrance into the destiny designed for us by God from all eternity. The reward of the traveller is to go on travelling, the solace of the searcher is to go on searching.

As this our final journey opens out and expands, we are, together with all whom we love and hold dear, bonded ever closer together

114

within Christ's mystical body. Nor are we led into some sort of pantheism as some pseudo-mystics suggest, because love differentiates. When we love and are loved, then the love that we receive enables us to grow into our true selves from the ruins that sin and selfishness made of us at the beginning of our journey. If this is true of human love, how much more is it true of Divine love? As we practise divine loving more and more, we are gradually permeated, penetrated, and possessed ever more fully by God's Love, not just in this world, but in the next world too. It was for this very purpose that God created us in His image and likeness from the beginning, with hearts therefore capable of endlessly expanding to receive in ever greater measure His infinite loving. And as the process continues, we become more ourselves than we ever were before.

As long as we are continually open to receive God's love, we are in a continuous progressive state of becoming the person God wanted us to be from the beginning. This is not only true of us, but also of those whom we love who travel with us. So, we continually rejoice at what infinite love is doing to us and to those whom we love. If we have unwittingly thought that our passport would lead us to Perfection, as to a new state of being in a specifically defined place, then we have been misled. It is a passport that leads us to the perfection which involves a deeper, fuller, and ever ongoing state of becoming our true selves, under the influence of the infinite loving of God our Father, our divine and ever devoted Dad who is in heaven.

He is our true home, the home in which He first conceived us, and the home for which our whole being has been yearning, within the infinite loving that constitutes the Three in One. For, as St Augustine put it, our hearts have been created for God alone and they will never rest until they rest in Him.

Post Scriptum

Early Christian Spirituality

Though it was released prior to *Passport to Perfection*, David Torkington's book, *Early Christian Spirituality* (formerly entitled *Family Spirituality*, published by Essentialist Press) is a perfect companion to those trying to live the practices taught within this book.

Early Christian Spirituality is not only deeply inspiring, but the work gives significantly greater details about the profound Mystical Spirituality first practised by Jesus Christ Himself before being introduced into the Early Church. In his Foreword to this book, Catholic author Kevin Wells noted that, "David Torkington is the world's foremost Mystical Theologian. You will find no better teacher this side of heaven. The pages before you are a synthesis of all he knows, of all God has spoken to the caverns of his heart. In this book, he has given to you seventy-five years of experience, study and untiring prayer for a single reason: He wants to reveal to you the manner in which God can seep into every corner of your life".

Early Christian Spirituality can be purchased directly from EssentialistPress.com, Amazon.com or from other good book shops who carry our works.

Addendum

A Pattern for Personal Prayer

To begin with you can use this pattern for daily prayer, but many people find that they eventually come to know the Blueprint off by heart, and they prefer to use their own words rather than the set prayers below.

Begin with Psalm sixty-nine with which St Benedict instructed his monks to start the divine office. Then it can be followed by the Glory Be, immediately followed by Psalm sixty-two.

> *O God, come to my aid*
> *O Lord, make haste to help me (Psalm 69).*
> *Glory be to the Father and to the son*
> *and to the Holy Spirit. Amen.*
>
> *O God, you are my God, for you I long;*
> *For you my soul is thirsting.*

118

My body pines for you
Like dry weary land without water (Psalm 62).

Morning Prayer

Say the Our Father and then using the Our Father as a memory jog, say the following prayers:

Our - Offering: – The Morning Offering

God, our Father, I wish to consecrate all that I say and all that I do to you in this forthcoming day, just as Jesus did every day of his life on earth. Please accept what I do so imperfectly and unite it with the perfect offering that Jesus continues to make to you in heaven and in every Mass that is celebrated on earth. I offer to you my joys and my sorrows, my successes as well as my failures, because these especially show how much I have need of you. I make my prayer in, with, and through Jesus in whom we all live and move and have our being. Amen.

Our - Union

Father, I know that the more your Holy Spirit draws me into your son Jesus, the more I am united to all who are within Him. I therefore ask Mary and Joseph, Peter and Paul and all the saints, especially those to whom I have a special devotion, to be with me now as I pray so that my prayers may be fortified by theirs. I also want to pray for all my family and friends and all who have asked me to pray for them. May they benefit from the day ahead that I wish to become a perfect prayer, as I offer all I say and do to you, through Jesus Christ Our Lord. Amen.

Our - Resolutions

Jesus, help me to review the day ahead to anticipate all that I should do, so that I can love God as you did through everything that I do, and love my neighbour too, as you love all of us. Help me to forgive my enemies as you forgave, as well as my friends. And give me the grace to seek forgiveness from those I have offended; and never to cease trying to be like you and to behave like you in all that I say and do. (Short pause to make resolutions for the day ahead).

Daily Prayer/Evening Prayer

Father - Faith

Father, I know and believe that you are all loving, that your love has been permanently transformed into human loving through the human nature of your son Jesus. I know and believe that His love is perpetually poised to possess me at this moment and at every moment. Penetrate and possess me now, permeate my whole being as I try to turn and remain open to receive you. Melt my heart of stone, re-make it and re-mould it, so that it can at all times be open to receive you. "For I, unless you enthral me, never shall be free, nor ever chaste except you ravish me" (John Donne). Amen.

Father - Abandonment

Father, you have freely chosen to share your own inner life and love with me now through Jesus, as a foretaste of the ecstatic joy that you have planned for me and for all who love you in heaven. As there is no limit to the way you have poured out your loving goodness and mercy on me, I can only totally abandon myself to you in return. I, therefore, solemnly consecrate every moment of every day to you and to your honour and glory, in and together with your son, Jesus Christ. Amen

Father - Thanksgiving

Father, although you are infinitely distant, you are infinitely near too, for you inhabit the inner marrow of my being. I thank you for being with me and for all you have given me today, for life itself and all and everyone that has made it worth living. Give me the grace to praise, honour, and thank you, as much as I am able and more than I am able, not just in words but in a life that I freely dedicate to you. Amen.

Father - Holy Communion

Jesus, at the Last Supper you promised to make your home in all who would obey your new commandments. Help me to obey them now and at every moment of my life. For when I love the Father and love my neighbour, as you did, there is nothing to stop you making your home in me and me making mine in you. Let the joy and the peace that comes from abiding in you suffuse all I say and do, so that others may be drawn into the Holy Communion that begins in this life and comes to its completion in the next. Amen.

(Now is the time to remain still and silent for a few moments of contemplation to relish what, or rather whom, we receive in this Holy Communion. A short prayer could be repeated gently whenever distractions threaten to draw the attention elsewhere. A prayer such as '*Come, Lord*' or '*Come, Lord Jesus*' would be ideal if not another short prayer of your choosing).

Father - Examination of Conscience

"Lord, that I may see," so that all that prevents you from making your home in me may be spirited away. Strengthen me to live the new commandments as you lived them, so that the same Holy Spirit who filled you, guided you, and raised you from the dead may do the same for me. Show me the sins that keep you out and give me the power to overcome them, for without you I have no power to do anything. Amen.

Father - Repentance

Father, I ask your forgiveness for the sins that have prevented you from possessing me as you would wish this day. (A short pause to review our behaviour in the past day.) I am deeply sorry for failing you yet again, and with your grace, I will never let my pride cause me to delay from turning back to you the moment I fall. Until I can love everyone as I should, help me to do them no harm and give me the sympathy and compassion of the person in whose footsteps I want to walk. Amen.

Conclude with an Our Father, a Hail Mary, and a Glory Be.

Night Prayer - A suggestion taken from an ancient tradition traced back to the Desert Fathers:

When you are in bed, say a short prayer and repeat it slowly and prayerfully. It may simply be the word, Jesus, or the full Jesus prayer: *Jesus Son of God, have mercy on me, a sinner.*

This prayer and others like it came to be used most particularly in the Eastern Christian Church with slow rhythmical breathing. It was not just a device for relaxation, but for reminding the believer of the all-pervading action of the Holy Spirit. The ancient Jews believed that the breath of believers was their life-principle, their spirit, so naturally they believed that God's breath was His life-principle, His Spirit. As a mark of respect, God's breath or His Spirit came to be called the Holy Spirit. So, deep rhythmic breathing that often accompanied short prayers of the heart helped remind Eastern Christians of the incoming Spirit who dwelt within them with ever increasingly power the more they prayed. It can be a reminder to us too, particularly when preparing for sleep.

The prayer *Come, Holy Spirit* can accompany the slow intake of breath followed by the prayer, *Conceive Christ in me*, as we breathe out. With the next breath, pray again *Come, Holy Spirit* followed by, *fill every part of me*, and again with the next breath, 'Come, Holy Spirit', followed by, *bring Christ to birth in me*. Then, the three prayers could be repeated again and again. Other short prayers could be used like, *Come, Lord*, or *Come, Lord Jesus,* or whatever short prayer you feel helps you best. When this practice becomes a habit, it can be far more effective than sleeping pills, and there are no side effects either.

Whenever you have finished trying to pray, be at peace. You have done the best you can. Now, leave the rest to God, remembering the words of St Padre Pio, "Pray, hope and don't worry."